Praise for *The Ultimate Guide to Power & Influence*

"Robert Dilenschneider's latest book on power and influence is a great read; practical and straightforward. 'Power through people' and 'networking is working' have always been my go-to timeless principles that Robert reinforces in this must read for business execs and entrepreneurs alike."

—Maggie Wilderotter, Chairman and CEO, Grand Reserve Inn

"Whatever your position in life, even if your ultimate ambition is not power or influence, reading *The Ultimate Guide to Power & Influence* is a smart way to success and self-fulfillment."

—Patrick Thomas, Verdi Consulting

"Public relations maven Bob Dilenschneider has done it again with a must-read new book on power and influence. His smart advice on networking, career pivoting, crisis management, and seeing around corners for trends makes the book a coach on the shelf for leaders and those who want to be."

—Glenn Hubbard, Russell L. Carson Professor of Economics and Finance, Columbia University

"*The Ultimate Guide to Power & Influence* is an enormous gift to existing and aspiring executives who intend to meaningfully impact the future trajectory of their organization. Bob Dilenschneider has had a front row seat for in excess of four decades to every major event that has impacted American business, and he has provided sage counsel to countless CEOs and executives as they have formulated their response to such events. His counsel transcends pure business advice and always balances reputational factors as well as family life balance. As a beneficiary of Bob's counsel over many years, I can attest to his wisdom."

—David L. Sokol, Chairman and CEO, Teton Capital, LLC

"One of my great pleasures in life was to get to know Bob. There is no other person I know who has more insight into the grooming of an effective leader, and the character and courage it takes to follow through. His insight on government and crisis management is second to none. This book is a perfect example of why Bob is truly the best at what he does. It covers all the bases, a must read."

—Ted Balestreri, Chairman and CEO, Cannery Row Company & The Inns of Monterey, Co-founder & CEO, The Sardine Factory Restaurant

The
ULTIMATE
GUIDE
to
POWER &
INFLUENCE

The
ULTIMATE
GUIDE
to
POWER &
INFLUENCE

Everything You Need to Know

Robert L. Dilenschneider

Matt Holt Books
An Imprint of BenBella Books, Inc.
Dallas, TX

Matt Holt is an imprint of BenBella Books, Inc.
10440 N. Central Expressway
Suite 800
Dallas, TX 75231
benbellabooks.com
Send feedback to feedback@benbellabooks.com

BenBella and *Matt Holt* are federally registered trademarks.

Printed in the United States of America
10 9 8 7 6 5 4 3 2 1

Library of Congress Control Number: 2022060007
ISBN 9781637742938 (hardcover)
ISBN 9781637742945 (electronic)

Copyediting by Lydia Choi
Proofreading by Madeline Grigg and Kellie Doherty
Indexing by WordCo Indexing Services, Inc.
Text design and composition by PerfecType, Nashville, TN
Cover design by Morgan Carr
Printed by Lake Book Manufacturing

This book is for Geoffrey and Peter, who should know and refine the points that follow.

CONTENTS

CONTENTS

INTRODUCTION

You have a choice. Keep doing what you did yesterday or adapt to a world that is changing every day. If you choose the second course, read this book.

You see, the world is changing at a faster pace than we could have imagined even a decade ago. By the time you finish reading what you're holding in your hand or is propped on your desk—whether it's a hardcover with paper pages or an electronic screen—things will be different. You have to keep up, or you'll be left behind.

Your life has real changes. Whatever you did twenty-four months ago, definitely five years ago—everything has changed. By the time you get to your next birthday, almost every element of your life will have transformed again.

You have to adapt and prepare for this.

But how do you prepare for the unknown? How do you prepare for a future that will bring innovations and circumstances not even dreamed of today? Think of how the future looked back in, say, the turn of the century. The iPhone alone revolutionized communication—and so much more—when it came out in 2007. Who would have thought our phones would be our cameras, and sophisticated ones at that, or instruments to order pizza digitally or pay bills or read newspapers or watch videos? It's mind-boggling. And something we now take for granted as we eagerly await new versions.

Starting right now, you have to get out ahead and anticipate what is coming. You need to do your research. You must be nimble.

This book will help you not only weather the changes but also thrive. And, I hope, lead to challenging yourself.

You will learn the secrets to attaining power and influence. You will learn how to use your status for the greater good. And ultimately, you will learn to be the best possible version of yourself.

This book is about your life and your future. Follow the steps, and you'll enjoy a better life.

The well-rounded individual makes little distinction between work and play, labor and leisure, the mind and body, education and recreation, love and religion. When you are doing work that provides satisfaction and personal fulfillment, it doesn't feel like work. It is part of the natural flow of your life. It's like moving effortlessly with the current in a river instead of fighting every inch to go upstream.

You will need a purpose for your work. And, importantly, you'll need to be mindful of a work–life balance.

Every chapter has something relevant for you, no matter your age or place in your career. Pick and choose what you need when you need it.

There are countless business books out there giving advice on just about everything. Some are quite good. But this book comes to you from decades of experience working with some of the most successful companies in the world—and the people who lead them.

I've been called the "Dean of American Public Relations Executives." Oftentimes my involvement as an international consultant comes at a time of crisis. I've led a multinational company as president and CEO of a major public relations firm, tripling its revenue. Thirty-plus years ago, I started my own Manhattan-based public relations firm, The Dilenschneider Group.

My firm, with offices in New York, Chicago, and Miami, provides strategic advice to Fortune 500 companies, as well as to leading families and individuals around the world. Our specialties range from mergers, acquisitions, and crisis communications to marketing, government affairs, international media, and a whole lot more.

Every day, business and political leaders come to me for advice. *Every day.*

This unique book is based on my years of experience and the lessons culled from scores of influential business leaders from various industries and backgrounds.

I care deeply about our country and became quite concerned with the eroding of civility in discourse. So I took action. In 2012, The Dilenschneider Group, along with the Hearst Corporation, initiated the Civility in America lecture series, which features many of the nation's leading thinkers from a wide variety of professions and provides a perspective on what must be done to restore civility. Speakers have spanned the likes of publishing executive Steve Forbes, Emmy-winning television journalist Deborah Norville, Yankees general manager Brian Cashman, bestselling author Barbara Taylor Bradford, former Texas governor Rick Perry, CNN historian Douglas Brinkley, and many more.

Each of these men and women is unique. And you are unique.

Find a way to make *your* mark.

That's what Arnold Donald did—he revolutionized the cruise-line industry after he became CEO and president in 2013 of Carnival Corporation & plc, the parent company of the flagship Carnival Cruise Line, Princess

Cruises, Holland America Line, Seabourn, P&O Cruises, Costa Cruises, AIDA Cruises, and Cunard.

He had been in semiretirement after leading Monsanto for about twenty years, then formed his own company. One of Donald's goals with Carnival was to bring the various brands together to share practices and strengthen the company.

"The brands have extensive communication, collaboration, and coordination, and they didn't have it before from a diversity standpoint," Donald told *USA Today* after stepping down in mid-2022 from the job he intended to hold for only three years but kept for triple that time. "The majority of our fleet now . . . is led by women."[1]

This emphasis on communication, collaboration, and coordination proved pivotal when the COVID-19 pandemic shut down the cruise industry for more than a year.

Donald raised the standards of people involved in the cruise-line industry. He is the kind of leader who dug in during the crisis and did for himself and others what had to be done.

By 2022, for the industry as a whole, COVID-19 testing of vaccinated passengers was eased, and several dozen new ships were introduced—some with features such as French chef Daniel Boulud's first restaurant on a ship. The Cruise Lines International Association predicts that by 2023, passenger numbers will surpass pre-pandemic levels.[2]

Influence means power, the power to make things happen. With power comes a great responsibility to use it wisely. You carry this obligation most of all to your family but also to your colleagues, community, social organizations, town, state, country—to humanity.

Have a mission, something you want to achieve. Know thyself and what you're good at. Know what's important to you—generally, it's what's closest to you.

Cyrus Freidheim could have pursued any number of ventures with success, but he had the self-awareness to realize what he really wanted to do—and how to do it.

I met Freidheim when we were both in Chicago, and we developed a good working relationship and friendship. At one point, he was likely to be the head of Booz Allen Hamilton, a leading management and information-technology consulting company based in Virginia. This would have been a prestigious position. But Freidheim said, "What the hell! I can do more if I don't have to be the top guy."

He became a consultant. One of his clients was the Sun-Times Media Group, which owned the *Chicago Sun-Times*. Freidheim set a goal to make the newspaper a must-read across Chicago. Another client was Chiquita Brands International, and along the way he served on fifteen corporate boards and twenty-plus not-for-profit boards. He wrote the book *Commit & Deliver*, published in 2021, with the subtitle *On the Frontlines of Management Consulting.*

Freidheim was successful, in part because he was inclusive and respectful. He would try to get everyone's point of view before making a decision. We were both members of The Chicago Club, and I would hear him greet the waiters there like long-lost friends. That's how he treated people. I never heard him say anything bad about anyone. Instead of embarrassing someone, he would simply ask, "Why not do it this way?"

Freidheim's admirable management style and business pursuits emanated from having the honesty to know himself and what was important to him.

Look at a newspaper and see how things change day to day. Look back a year ago, even a month. Every aspect of the world has shifted.

Climate change is happening with cataclysmic weather—droughts, floods—throughout the world. The political arena is a moving target. Democracy is under siege, and venerable institutions are assailed.

Forces are rearranging outside the United States. Russia invaded Ukraine in 2022 as the world watched and NATO drove sanctions. China is pushing to become the leading economic power in the world; Iran and North Korea are unsettling, to say the least.

Wealth is changing. Even currency is changing, with people now doing transactions with cryptocurrency.

The media is changing as outlets merge and broadcast and streaming options explode. Some cable "news" shows are decidedly partisan and increasingly wield enormous influence over large blocks of the public.

Science is changing. A pandemic killed millions worldwide and disrupted economies as scientists frantically searched for a vaccine. Paradoxically, a sizable portion of the population distrusts the vaccines and refuses to take any. Thus, the virus still roams, replicates, kills.

Business is changing. A lot of small start-ups are assuming a role in America they didn't have before. Behemoth corporations must be agile and quick; some, such as General Electric, are splitting and divesting. The top-down patriarchy management style of the Industrial Age is archaic.

The pandemic affected the culture of corporations and the workplace. Employees, especially young ones, reassessed priorities and began looking for places to work with values aligned with their own, such as a commitment to authentic inclusion and/or sustainability. The need to work from home during the shutdown for non-frontline positions led to the desire for hybrid situations instead of the traditional day-to-day in an office with others.

The need for social change is emphasized with marches and movements, such as Black Lives Matter and #MeToo. Public statues of former heroes are removed from civic squares as history is reexamined through a shifting cultural lens. Some industry leaders were toppled under accusations of sexual abuse: think Roger Ailes of Fox News or Harvey Weinstein, the Hollywood producer.

These forces also are demanding reform in the corporate world.

Change is pervasive and rapid.

What has staying power? Will the latest TikTok influencer be known a generation from now? Five years from now? In a world where it's always onto something new, something previously not imagined, you want endurance.

You have to figure out how to understand and get through such a world. And not only get through it—but thrive.

If you can navigate change, you'll be successful personally.

————————

The art of influence is defining, realizing, and gradually strengthening your personal agenda.

How should you position yourself to attain power and influence, what do you do once you get it, and how do you keep it?

This book will show the way.

When I talk about motivation, some assume financial gain is the primary impetus for seeking influence and power. It is as though all the facets of pursuing a career—and a well-lived life—funnel to the purpose of amassing wealth. But that is not so! Money will come to you if you have an idea. But if money is your sole goal, go to Wall Street and Goldman Sachs.

Many don't pay attention to money but still become successful. Money is not the size of your success. It is one indicator. Do you move the needle? Improve society? Are you in a position to make things happen so that everyone wins? Money is not attached to these things. It doesn't have to be your motivator.

"Remember that the only purpose of money is to get you what you want, so think hard about what you value and put it above money."[3] That advice comes from one of the smartest and wealthiest people in the country, Ray Dalio, the founder of Bridgewater Associates, a leading asset-management firm, in his excellent book *Principles*.

As a manager, though, you should pay your employees fairly, he advises. "By being generous or at least a little north of fair with others I have enhanced both our work and our relationships and most people have responded in kind. As a result, we have gained something even more special than money in the form of mutual caring, respect, and commitment."[4]

Where do ideas come from? Do the best ideas come from Harvard or Yale? Some do, but some come from Slippery Rock. At one point, Harvard and Yale had a lock, but not now. No matter who you are or where you're from, there's no reason you can't have a great idea.

Pete Cashmore was only nineteen when he had an idea for a business—and he launched it from his bedroom. That was in 2005. Today, Mashable is a digital media platform with a focus on technology, a news website, and an entertainment company averaging more than 22 million page views a month.

"I'm very much a creative person, but you've got to do the follow-through," he said in an interview published in Toronto's *Globe and Mail*. "A lot of people start out with an exciting thing and they want to take over the world, but really the people who do take over the world have a good plan of how to get there and the steps along the way."[5]

A plan, your personal and professional road map, is essential. It must be flexible and aspirational. Dream big. How to do this will come later in this book.

In trying to get ahead, if you were to jump on every idea you have, you would be overwhelmed. Pick three to four things, and then figure out how you want to do them and who can help you. Once you've accomplished the first three or four, pick another three ideas. Repeat again and again.

When Indra Nooyi joined PepsiCo as an executive in 1994, the company was already successful. By the time she became its CEO twelve years later, she knew an ambitious plan was required to move a company rooted in selling soda and chips to a "full-throttle effort to make and market more healthy products,"[6] as she relates in her book *My Life in Full: Work, Family, and Our Future.*

This would be enough for anyone to tackle. But Nooyi, the first woman of color who is also an immigrant to run a Fortune 500 company, also saw in business a disconnect with work and family life—and she wanted to fix it.

"We must address the work and family conundrum by focusing on our infrastructure around 'care' with an energy and ingenuity like never before," she writes. "We should consider this a moonshot, starting with ensuring that every worker has access to paid leave, flexibility, and predictability to help them handle the ebb and flow of work and family life, and then moving fast to develop the most innovative and comprehensive childcare and eldercare solutions that our greatest minds can devise."[7]

It will be up to you. "The fundamental role of a leader," Nooyi says, "is to look for ways to shape the decades ahead, not just react to the present, and to help others accept the discomfort of disruptions to the status quo."[8]

So think about your ideas. What makes *you* tick?

State your objective as clearly as you can. Work on two or three critical sentences with as few words as possible that define where you want to go. Make them robust. Keep it succinct, like an elevator pitch. Most never take the time to write down their objectives. That's a mistake. Some write paragraphs, even chapters. That's not smart, either. People will become confused or lose interest.

How can your idea be exciting enough to keep you going? How can it move society, your social circle, or even people you don't know? For the person who gets this and has some degree of drive, their ideas can be a matter of one plus one equals three. That's who this book is for.

In this book, you will gain insight into promoting your ideas through networking, building personal connections, and harnessing social media to work for you. Some chapters will resonate with a particular point in your career, such as when to pivot your direction and how to do it. You'll also learn how to protect your reputation.

I consider the chapter on communication a must-read for everyone. Effective communication is at the heart of good management. If you are communicating effectively, you will get positive recognition from the audiences you are trying to influence. People will know that what you are doing is right and that you are doing it in the right way. When you get positive recognition, your influence grows. You are perceived as competent, effective, worthy of respect—in other words, powerful.

As you can deduce, the first part of the book centers on building your power and influence step by step. The second part pertains to keeping your influence, handling your power in times of crisis, and predicting trends.

And, as promised, you will see the "why" and "how" of sharing your power.

You won't want to miss the chapter on how to become a memorable manager. Or the one on how to make the right mistakes.

———

"Inclusion" has become a buzzword lately, but it is crucial that you know how to create an inclusive atmosphere in the workplace—and to do it authentically.

Jim Farley, CEO of Ford Motor Company, has practiced inclusion by seeking ideas from all levels since he took the reins in 2020.

Farley listened to a devoted band of fans of the discontinued Bronco SUV within the company and allowed them to propose a wildly successful redesign of the vehicle. He also gave free rein to Linda Zhang, a Ford engineer, to oversee the development of the F-150 Lightning electric truck.

Though driven to succeed, Farley is also social-minded. During the pandemic, Ford retooled factories to produce fifty thousand ventilators and provided 120 million face masks for its dealers to distribute in their communities. Under Farley, Ford has also committed to a redevelopment of Detroit's abandoned downtown train station and surrounding community.

And he is constantly looking forward. He's invested billions in electric vehicles and a self-driving car program called BlueCruise.

Today's most successful executives, who have built their teams wisely, do not think twice about asking subordinates, "What do you think?" They understand that such a question is not a sign of weakness or insecurity but a tool to make their own performance and that of their company better.

Every day, ask yourself: How have I learned from my mistakes? If you are taking risks, as you should, you'll make mistakes. Don't waste a mistake! Learn from it.

With the dizzying forward pace of everything from technology to communication, one element must remain constant—your values. I cannot tell you what your values should be; they are personal to you. But among them should be the commitment to helping others. That is how society functions best and how the human race improves.

Influence is about who you are, not just what you do. Character will define you.

In leadership, you will need to make critical decisions every day. You can't put a finger to the wind to see which way it's blowing; you'll just get buffeted about. Polls only go so far. You must have your own moral compass in place.

My father, S. J. Dilenschneider, taught me that important lesson from an early age. He ran the *Columbus Citizen* in Columbus, Ohio, a leading voice in the community and the newspaper of record.

One day, a prominent local businessman died by suicide. Should the newspaper publish a story? He had been a public figure.

Dad said, "Run it."

His phone rang. He went to the basement, where he took all of his hard calls in those days. A youngster, I hid behind some stacks of old reports down there and eavesdropped.

"You run that story, and we're taking all of our advertising out of the newspaper!" The call was from an executive of the Cussins & Fearn department store, a large retail business in the city, where the local businessman had worked. Naturally, its ties to the community ran deep. But so did the newspaper's. The editor had to be fair; no favors when it came to what went in the news—or stayed out of it.

My father was steadfast; the short news item of the suicide was published. That day, as promised, the store pulled all of its advertising. It was a huge blow to the paper's income.

About ten days went by, and there was a knock at my dad's office door. Fred Lazarus Jr. walked in with a Japanese attendant who laid out a formal tea service. "I understand that Cussins took out all of its advertising," Lazarus said. "Well, we're going to double our commitment and drive them out of business!" And that's exactly what he did. F&R Lazarus & Company, which was founded in 1851, later became Federated Department Stores, and in 2007 was renamed Macy's for the chain it had acquired in 1994; it now is the world's largest fashion-goods retailer.

If you do the right thing, you're never going to have a problem. If you do the right thing, you might become hugely successful. If you do the right thing, you're giving lessons to others to do the right thing. On the flip side, if you do the wrong thing, people will scorn you. Doing the right thing is critically important.

Okay, let's get started on your personal path to power and influence. This will be exciting—and possibly life changing.

CHAPTER 1

Taking First Steps
Critical to
Your Future

This book is about you and how you might progress in life. Follow the rules and you will do well. Ignore them at your peril.

Let's start with: "Who are *you?*"

Marquis de Lafayette asks this of Alexander Hamilton in the hit Broadway play *Hamilton*. And this is the key question to ask yourself before you start down the path to acquiring power and influence and making your life what you deserve.

This book is written for you. The goal is to give you ideas and to help you think about how to make your life better. Why? Because if your life is better, then everyone you come into contact with will be better. And that is an achievement.

It is important to know who you are and where you want to go—at any age or stage of your career. So, what do you stand for? What risks are you willing to take?

The answers will be—and should be—different for each of us. The answers will lead you to knowing and making the most of your life and your leadership style. A crucial component of being an influential leader is *authenticity*.

You have to be honest almost to a fault. If you're not honest with yourself, it's going to be a big problem.

Jack Welch, the storied CEO of General Electric (GE), knew he was different from most CEOs. The title of one of his bestsellers, *Jack: Straight from the Gut*, makes that clear. No artifice. He knew who he was and was true to himself, even if that seemed unconventional for a CEO.

He encouraged people to take risks, chances. If the outside world was changing faster than the company was, failure was certain, he believed. There was no standing still, even for a public corporation paying healthy stock dividends. Though GE was one of the most successful corporations at the time, Welch took a risk and set up GE Capital under Gary Wendt, one of the best executives in the company.

GE Capital went on to become one of the most important financial institutions in the world.

Welch didn't try to be like any other figure. He was himself; he was authentic, like him or not. He was successful.

So, tell me about yourself. You've probably been asked that many times at a dinner party, or at a job interview, or maybe when you look in the mirror. Likely the answer varies for each situation. But think about your first, unfiltered response. Do you start with your relationships ("I am a mother of two . . .")? Your career ("I've been in the technology field for a dozen years and have seen a lot of changes . . .")? Your personal achievements ("I ran my first marathon in New York City last November and finished . . .")? Your interests ("I'm a foodie. I love to cook but also love to try new restaurants . . .")? Your history ("I went to Notre Dame and still try to get back at least once in the fall for a football game . . .")?

All of these answers may be true, but do they define who you are? Recall another well-known question from *Hamilton*: "What do you stand for?"

Know your values. Be ready to advance and defend them if necessary. Be true to them.

Contemplate what it means—to you—to be a good human being. Do you live your life and pursue your career with integrity?

"The first true step of leadership is understanding yourself, how others perceive you, and learning to use your skills effectively. And you may not like doing it, but that all starts with a journey of personal reflection and growth,"[1] advises Dan Stifter of the Henry W. Bloch

School of Management at the University of Missouri–Kansas City.

Self-awareness, Stifter says, is one of the four pillars of emotional intelligence (along with empathy, self-management, and social skills) and must come first. "'[Knowing] thyself' isn't about being master of your domain, it's about truly understanding how your behaviors are perceived by others. Want to be an effective leader? Find out how others see you."[2]

How to do that? Take a good look inside yourself. It is important to make an assessment of who you are, and that can begin with the seemingly simple step of writing on a piece of paper or tapping keys on your laptop.

Regardless of the method, you need to take the time to write things down and say, "Who am I? I am a man of x number of years, a woman of x number of years, a person of x number of years. I have these interests, I have these goals"—everybody should have goals—"and I have a means of reaching these goals. I have the ability to identify and reach people to help me. I have friends. And I know who my adversaries are—I know their arguments, I know how to deal with them. I am a loyal person." And so on.

Understand all the qualities you think could shape your environment—or you. Ignore or fend off what compromises you. Build from this foundation, and you will realize your potential.

You can even google yourself. Is what you see accurate? If not, make corrections.

You are perceived in part based on what you do outside of your work life. To which organizations and non-profits do you contribute your time, your money? There's not a person in America who doesn't receive a barrage of requests for donations every day in emails, social-media posts, even your mailbox. And remember, some of those can be part of a public record, such as the political candidates to whom you contribute.

You must make judgments.

What you stand for has to be more than a "like" on a social-media post or sharing a meme. You must have substance.

Rita Moreno knew she had to be true to herself, even though that came with great personal sacrifice. The first Latina to win an Academy Award for Best Actress (for her role as Maria in the original *West Side Story*), she became typecast to play "the house ethnic," she told NPR in 2013, reflecting on her early years in movies.[3] She wasn't going to compromise her artistic talent; she didn't want to be a stereotype. At the height of a marketable career, she took seven years off from making movies. The result? True roles, fulfilling roles, came to her. Along with a Grammy, a Tony, two Emmys, and a Peabody Career Achievement Award.

How you think about yourself might be very different from how others see you. How you see yourself is one version; how you actually are could be another; how others think of you could be completely different. You need to understand all of these versions.

Be honest with yourself. You might fashion yourself as an art aficionado, but in reality you can't tell a Matisse from a Basquiat. And others may see you as pretentious.

Align those different versions—educate yourself on French painters and set a goal that directs you to authenticity. If you couldn't care less about French painters, then focus on something else that genuinely interests you.

You need to see how others think about you. If you can't master how you're really seen by other people, you're going to have a problem.

Granted, it's hard to get outside of yourself. But here are three steps you can take:

1. Ask a close friend for an honest assessment.
2. Look at what's been public about you. Have you been quoted in a newspaper, a blog, or a podcast? What is the echo?
3. Consider: When you give a speech (of any kind) or just talk to people around you, what questions do people ask?

If you can do the above, you'll begin to chart who you are. You'll improve your chances of achieving something.

I won't go so far to say, like Socrates, that an unexamined life is not worth living, but I will draw the parallel that an examined life gives meaning.

You shouldn't proceed on anything until you know who you are. Ask yourself: Does my life reflect my values? Do I act with integrity?

Once that's determined, who do you want to be? Find your passion, a combination of your deepest interests and your best abilities. Focus your key decisions here.

Rachel Carson loved both science and writing. She possessed a unique ability to make technical information understandable and attractive to general readers while never dumbing it down. From her combined passion, she changed the world with her 1962 book, *Silent*

Spring. This is not an exaggeration. Her book focused public attention on the dangers to the environment caused by DDT and other pesticides. It led to the establishment of the US Environmental Protection Agency in 1970.

This one person made others concerned about the environment, ecology, and the climate and heightened awareness of the interconnectedness of human, plant, and animal life. Talk about influence!

Maria Tallchief realized she had to be true to her passion—dance—and thus to herself. She loved music and dancing as a child growing up in the Osage Nation in Oklahoma. She knew Chopin as well as she knew the rattling of gourds and the tinkling of bells, doing pliés as naturally as the side-to-side shuffling typical of Osage women dancers. By the time she was seventeen, her career as a ballerina was underway. Most notably associated with the New York City Ballet, she became the first Native American prima ballerina. She revolutionized American ballet through her immense physical talents and devotion to excellence.

When Tallchief retired from performing, she continued to follow her passion through, among other achievements, founding the Chicago City Ballet, where she served as an artistic director.

As you sort through your passions, your talents, and your values, ask yourself how much you care about particular institutions—schools and education, the military, your church, the people in your company, the president of the United States. Think about it as you work toward defining who you are and what you stand for.

Look into the pit of your stomach and ask: "Who do I want to be like?" Who is your hero, historic or present? Why? Take stock of the qualities you would like to emulate. Take a holistic approach. Maybe this person reflects the qualities that are important to you and that you want to have. Or maybe this person is honest or doesn't try to hurt anybody. This person might understand the world around them. Perhaps this person picked a spot where their energy makes a difference. It could be that if you're involved with them, you'll make a difference.

Have heroes. You can even take individual elements from a lot of well-known people and figure out what makes them heroes. But ultimately, be uniquely you.

Consider the obstacles you've faced. Maybe you didn't go to an Ivy League university; maybe you grew up in poverty; maybe you've had to struggle to get to where you are. But circumstances need not define you, and they need not limit your future.

At Mayer, Brown & Platt (now Mayer Brown LLP), a powerhouse international law firm headquartered in Chicago, recruiting often was from second-tier schools when I represented them. Why? Because they knew those graduates would work hard to show they were as good as those with degrees from Yale or Harvard.

Gabrielle Bonheur Chanel was born in a poorhouse and grew up in an orphanage. But she rose above that. She did it bit by bit by bit. She went from being a milliner to liberating women's fashion. She did it by involving others and taking things to the next level. Coco Chanel went on to become one of the most acclaimed fashion designers and set style and trends around the world. Her "little black dress" remains a staple today.

"My life didn't please me, so I created my life," she said. And so can you.

Norman Mineta, the son of Japanese immigrants, spent two years of his childhood in a World War II internment camp in the United States. Many could be forgiven for thinking it unlikely that this child would one day grow up to receive the Presidential Medal of Freedom, the nation's highest civilian honor. Mineta didn't let his years in the internment camp hold him back, but he also didn't forget. That experience contributed to his character. He broke racial barriers when he became the first Asian American mayor of San Jose, then became a federal cabinet secretary under two presidents, a Democrat and a Republican. He was the secretary of commerce for President Bill Clinton and the secretary of transportation for President George W. Bush. He is most well known for his response to the terrorist attacks on September 11, 2001; he ordered the grounding of all civilian aircraft, the first such order given in US aviation history.

Sometimes it's our experiences that propel us in a certain direction. When Janet Jensen was twenty-five, she was sexually assaulted while on a morning run. She turned around an intensely disturbing experience to become one of the nation's top advocates against all forms of sexual violence. She eventually founded the Jensen Project, where, as executive director, she strategically aligns "stakeholders with the best avenues for sustainable investments, creating impactful partnerships that build a better future for vulnerable and traumatized individuals,"4 her website states.

Jensen "advocated for critical changes in health care, which eventually led to the establishment of the first public hospital trained to receive and treat victims of sexual assault in Texas," as just one example of what she has accomplished. Additionally, she "became a frequent speaker on college and university campuses across the country, sharing her personal story of trauma and resilience and promoting an environment of compassion, empathy, and support for survivors."[5] Rather than defeated, Jensen became empowered and has accomplished much good for others.

Ray Dalio's elementary school teachers would probably be surprised at where he is in business today. He calls himself a "worse-than-ordinary student" in his book *Principles*.

"I didn't like school, not just because it required a lot of memorization, but because I wasn't interested in most of the things that my teachers thought were important,"[6] he writes. But he discovered what did interest him—investing—and pursued it with determination and passion. Dalio formed Bridgewater Associates out of his two-bedroom apartment in New York City. Today, that company is the world's largest hedge fund, and in 2022, he ranked in *Forbes*'s list of the top thirty billionaires in the United States.

"What I have seen," he writes in *Principles*, "is that the happiest people discover their own nature and match their life to it."[7]

———

When you know yourself, you can withstand pressure to follow other's expectations.

John Finn built up Gardner, Inc., into one of the largest parts distributors for the outdoor power-equipment industry. The privately owned family business is hugely successful, with five distribution centers covering the United States.

But Mike Finn, John's son, had a different idea. He didn't want to be part of that organization; it didn't speak to him.

Mike actually wrote out on a yellow legal pad who he wanted to be and what qualities he wanted to reflect. How could he get to where he wanted to go?

His father naturally kept after him—"You'll be a pillar in the community," he said. "People will look up to you." All of that is good, and certainly the company provided a worthwhile service. But it wasn't what Mike wanted to do.

Mike made a list of people who could help him and how. His list spanned about twenty. Over the course of three to four years, he went to each individual.

He formed his own company, Chesapeake Realty Co., a real-estate development and management company, and ended up playing a major role in society. Today, he travels the world, and he never would have been able to do that if he had stayed with Gardner. His dreams and desires would have been unfulfilled.

He went to the edge of the cliff and stepped off. Sometimes, that's what you have to do.

Be honest with yourself.

Be authentic.

Be you.

You don't have to be a big cheese in people's minds, but you do have to be genuinely aligned with who you are.

Maybe you think this is simplistic—maybe you think you know who you are and are skimming ahead. But believe me, doing this basic work and introspection will give you the foundation for all else to come.

With this self-knowledge springs the next question: Why do I want influence? This is not a "duh" question! With influence comes power, and you must stop to consider how you want to use it. Distill your response to a few sentences. Whatever your answer, be sure an element of the commonweal is there. You are not alone on this planet. Anyone who is out only for themselves will end up eventually alone, even among hundreds in, say, your company.

Many years ago, I encountered a man named Don who cared only about himself. He was determined to get to the top and did not care who he stepped on to do it. Well, everyone around him realized this in short order and stopped cooperating with him. When he would threaten individuals, the whole room would respond negatively to him. I don't know where Don is today, but he is not at the top of the company. I hope he has learned and changed his ways.

Examine what motivates you. And then set goals. Make them as precise as possible. "I want to be the president of a company by the time I'm forty" is fine. But to be able to effectively take steps toward that goal, you need to be more exact. "I want to be the president of my own start-up brokerage company with assets of $800 million by the time I'm forty" is much better. That gets you in a position to break your goal down into manageable steps.

A helpful acronym for goal setting is SMART: Specific, Measurable, Achievable, Relevant, and Time-Bound.

Many companies use this strategy for annual performance reviews because it is targeted and it works.

Start writing down the steps you need to take for three goals. Too many at once, and you'll be scattered. Too few, and you're not pushing yourself enough.

If you want something badly, you'll need to figure out what the first step toward getting it is and, if achieved, what the following step is going to be—and all the subsequent steps until you reach your goal.

Ron Zier, vice president of public affairs for the pharmaceutical company Warner–Lambert before it was subsumed by Pfizer, did this methodically and effectively.

Something would come up and he would always say, "Well, how are we going to do this?" We'd sit around and discuss, and he then would talk about steps to achieve the goal. It could be as simple as writing an annual report. The steps included deciding who will do it. "How will we get illustrations? How will it support the CEO? What kind of words, tone, should be used?" And inevitably if we went step by step, we'd achieve the goal.

As you start taking this important first step, take the time to reflect and to plan.

"Who are *you*?" can be one of the most exciting questions you will ever answer.

CHAPTER 2

Networking:
You Have to Do It

Networking is an overworked word. Many talk about it and abuse it. Few understand it or know how to do it or what it can mean.

Ask Frank Bennack about networking, and he'll tell you that building relationships can make all the difference in leading a company to unparalleled success. The CEO of the Hearst Corporation for more than thirty years, Bennack helped the privately held company become the multimedia towering force it is today. Consumers know Hearst through brands such as Oprah's *O* magazine, the *San Francisco Chronicle*, and the Lifetime cable channel.

One of Bennack's most remarkable achievements was negotiating a 20 percent stake in ESPN, a fledging sports network then in 1990, for $167 million. Now the network is worth billions.

How did the opportunity for investment happen? Through relationships.

Bennack was on the board of Allied Stores with Leonard Goldenson, the CEO of ABC, who also cofounded United Cerebral Palsy, a nonprofit that Bennack supported. "I think it was our shared values that led us to become friends,"[1] Bennack writes in his memoir, *Leave Something on the Table*. From that core relationship and through the labyrinth of multiple mergers and acquisitions, Bennack ended up on the receiving end of this call from Daniel Burke, then the CEO of Capital Cities/ABC: "A piece of ESPN is available. What do you think?"

Burke didn't call everyone. He called one person: Frank Bennack. Because of personal relationships and shared pro bono activities, "they thought we spoke a common language and had common values,"[2] Bennack writes in his memoir chapter aptly titled "It's Not Who You Know. It's How You Know Them. And How They Know You."

"Because stock market analysts have suggested ESPN is now worth $30 billion or substantially more, Hearst's ability to buy 20 percent of the company for $167 million is sometimes called 'the deal of the century,' though that might just be a bit of an exaggeration," Bennack continues. "This is not an exaggeration: Our pivot to cable networking was the single largest triumph in Hearst's modern history. And the most significant: Our cable partnership—Lifetime, A&E, and The History Channel—and the investment in ESPN have been more responsible for where the company is today financially than any other acquisition or launch in the company's history."[3]

This will be one of the most practical chapters you will read, with the potential to influence your career heights—and your life.

Networking is an art. You can join a network or build your own. The way it works best is when everyone has the chance to benefit.

Networks abound—your local chamber of commerce, Toastmasters International, Business Network International. Civic-minded service organizations, such as Rotary International or Lions Club International, can also be opportunities for networking. Nearly every industry has a related organization, such as the Society of Professional Journalists, where connections are made while promoting the shared objectives of the group. Networks can be quite specific—Lean In Circles, for example, are small peer groups in which businesswomen (and men) "meet regularly to learn and grow together,"[4] according to the homepage for Lean In, cofounded by Sheryl Sandberg, author of *Lean In: Women, Work, and the Will to Lead* and former COO of Facebook, now called Meta.

Choose your network wisely. Look for common interests, if you'd like, but also look for opportunities to meet contacts outside of your usual circle. Find a fit where you can do some good—with impact. Think about how you will do it; plan in advance. Avoid spreading yourself too thin. Find a way to focus your talent and energies. Make sure you don't do another ten things just for the sake of doing them.

While I prefer in-person networks for initial contacts, social-media sites such as LinkedIn, with more than 600 million users, can also be useful platforms for making connections.

When you are networking, remember that your purpose is to make contacts and build career, and possibly lifelong, relationships. You are not there, hat in hand, seeking a job. That may come eventually, but networking is not a one-way street. Have patience. The people you connect with need to come away thinking about what you could do for them, rather than the other way around.

Therefore, focus on what you have to offer. Research industries and leaders you are likely to meet. Have something to talk about with them that will convey your knowledge and interest. And most of all—*listen.*

The most successful people I know have their own networks, which they cultivate like a precious rose garden.

You need to find a way to form your own network so that those involved feel like they're getting something, too.

It's never too soon to set up your own network. In fact, young professionals should be collecting theirs right now. I started mine early in my degree pursuit at Notre Dame. It's also not too late if you're already established in your career. Your personal network can lead the way to greater heights.

Of course, this requires much more effort.

Bonnie McElveen-Hunter is a master at cultivating a network. With her varied roles as the first female chair of the American Red Cross's board of governors, the founder and CEO of Pace Communications, and the former US ambassador to Finland, her network of contacts is vast. For a less organized person, it would be unwieldy. But I saw firsthand how McElveen-Hunter manages when she joined me for lunch at a private club in midtown Manhattan many years ago.

Two of her assistants set up at a table nearby and monitored incoming messages from their laptops and cell phones. They managed priorities, and if a message needed immediate attention, they signaled their boss. One of those messages that day at lunch was from the White House; McElveen-Hunter quickly and discreetly responded without a fuss.

The trick to making an extensive network productive is knowing how to manage it. In a seventeen-to-eighteen-hour workday, there are countless people with whom you can stay in touch. You must prune your list but never cut people off entirely. Keep adding to your list. By adding people to your network, more opportunities are created for you. One way to manage your growing list is to make categories—contacts in the energy industry, the media, the nonprofit fields, for example.

Cultivate your network and keep your name out there through tools such as newsletters, letters to the editor, and op-eds. Make them informative, useful, succinct. Avoid overpowering the inbox, however. Any of us in business receive more emails in an hour than we could possibly read, even if that's all we did all day long. Make your message a must-read.

Networking is an ongoing process, not a one-and-done activity. You may think the purpose of your network is to grow your business, makes sales, recruit, or be recruited. But the truth is that it's about building relationships.

"In a world of social media and digital engagement, it is easy to overlook the remarkable efficacy of personal relationships," notes Don Spetner, a senior corporate adviser for Weber Shandwick Worldwide, in a piece written for the USC Annenberg School for Communication and Journalism. "The simple truth is relationships are almost as important as competence when it comes to climbing the corporate ladder."[5]

I like to think of networking in terms of "favor banks"—coined by Tom Wolfe in his novel *The Bonfire of the Vanities*. The book is satire, but Wolfe's point about favor banks remains illustrative. It captures an essential element in how the world of influence works.

"It's an efficient and time-worn system," writes Spetner. "It's also one of the most effective engines for advancing a career."[6]

Here's how it works: You make a "deposit" into the virtual favor bank, and later you will inevitably make a "withdrawal." When you make that withdrawal, it's important to do so elegantly and graciously so that everyone wins.

Let's say you're called to assess a candidate for a senior management job at an up-and-coming manufacturing firm. You provide a strong recommendation and are told she's at the top of the list. Fine. Now leverage that by immediately calling the candidate and telling her she's likely to get the job. Who do you suppose the candidate will think helped cinch the position?

Get credit for your favors this way.

Look for favors you can do. Continually pay attention to both sides of the ledger. Constantly look for favors that don't cost you anything. Who are the powerful people who feel antagonistic toward your business? I'm talking about special-interest leaders, columnists, politicians— anyone who can be a big-league aggravation. It may sound counterintuitive, but without undermining your business objectives or compromising ethics, do every possible favor you can for those people. It's done every day by top managers in the Fortune 500. Deposit regularly and heavily in the favor bank.

Figure out realistically whom you need and who needs you. Every time you confront a problem or launch a program, create an agenda for change. Next to each point, mark down which of the people who need you who could help make that change or resolution easier, more effective, or less expensive. People will do plenty for you. Most will even do it without a fee if you make two things clear: you don't intend to pay a fee for the service, and you really appreciate what they are doing. The favor must be reasonable, of course.

There are two kinds of balances you can draw on in the favor bank. The first is your personal account—the balance you build up by doing favors for others. The other is your corporate account, the balance you get for your company or organization by simply being in your position. No manager should impose on their company's favor-bank account before checking with the CEO or a top officer, however. It's at that level that balances are kept. The brass may think you have a great idea, but not checking it out with them first could cost you your career. Be smart.

Maintain a good "credit rating." Look for ways to maneuver the good with the not so good. What do I mean by that? For example, I might need a powerful institution like the Council on Foreign Relations to do me a favor. Say the finance minister from a Scandinavian country wants to speak at a prestigious US forum, but his message is rather routine. Simply put, I need someone to help eat the loss. Usually, I can get the job done. How? I will feed the organization something good in advance. A top economist calls me and says they're ready with a new slant on the economy. I contact a trend-setting publication and promise them an exclusive interview. I'll also go out of my way to secure another, hotly sought-after speaker for the council to make up for the ho-hum one.

Leading publications and organizations understand the unwritten rule. That's how you can keep your credit rating so it can withstand the occasional hits.

Support the rainmakers—those people who are capable of bringing new clients to a business. When Rabbi Arthur Schneier, one of the most influential people in New York and a human-rights activist, called me on a Sunday afternoon and asked whether the company where I worked at the time would help lead an earthquake-relief effort in a country on the border of Europe and Asia, it took me just one second to say yes. First, it was the right and humane thing to do. Second, it paid off handsomely in how the company was regarded. And third, it answered a rainmaker's call. If you want to maintain an active balance at the favor bank, jump when a rainmaker calls.

Deposit "intellectual capital" on the way up. Senior executives get a lot of mileage in their community through leveraging their company's contribution program. But what if you're just a young manager without a wad of money to give away? Are there ways to build up your personal account in the favor bank? Indeed there are. It's called trading in intellectual capital. Let's say you are a rising executive, and you want to make your impact felt with a politician. You know that you can't make a heavyweight financial contribution. But can you help them in designing their fundraising strategy? Can you spend your evening hours researching a particular topic so they can write a blockbuster speech? Just be sure the candidate's positions won't bring embarrassment to your company.

Your community hospital can't afford a financial-analysis function, but you hear that the trustees (who are also the most powerful community leaders) blame serious operating problems on a lack of good analysis. Can you step in and offer your expertise pro bono to troubleshoot the problem?

For managers at every level, there is a way to leverage intelligence and ingenuity for impact far beyond your apparent rank. Sweat-equity staff work is often the way to tone up the influence of a manager on the come.

Advertise your favor-bank balance. In a speech, you might hear an executive say, "When the local elementary schools needed Chromebooks for remote learning, we were glad to donate some to help equalize education. It was nothing less than an investment in the community and our children." This soft-sell advertisement amplifies power and influence. Of course, this must be done discreetly and with caution so as to not oversell. And most of all, it has to be true!

Be responsive, never offensive. Though it might not be today, someday you might need a prominent executive to go to bat for you. Every time you offend someone, you create a potential foe who may one day block your admission to the "club"—that circle of influential people at any given level. In general, and in every way, it's better to be responsive, not offensive.

Networking in every form comes down to building and maintaining relationships. Find ways that work for you—it will likely be an amalgam of in-person groups, professional social-media sites, and the favor bank.

Samuel Hyman is a pro at nudging people outside of their usual circles. A business and civic leader in western Connecticut, the former head of a local NAACP chapter, and a board member of a prominent hospital and other organizations, Hyman commands respect. He invites people, maybe a dozen or so who don't know each other, to meet for lunch in a private area of a local restaurant. He makes detailed introductions one by one; he is the link between them. Those gathered are a small part of Hyman's network, the fortunate beneficiaries of his generosity to widen their contacts.

Always look for ways to share, to build relationships in your own authentic way.

CHAPTER 3

The Power of the Personal Connection

The self-made person is an icon in the American psyche. But it is a myth.

While personal responsibility is important, if you think you can be successful all on your own, you're mistaken. Relationships are key in business and in life.

In this chapter, you will learn how to make meaningful connections with people that can boost your success in business and ultimately enrich your life.

Keep in mind, we're not talking about self-serving calculations. I believe people have a need to connect with each other—and that became dramatically clear during the COVID-19 pandemic when social opportunities were curtailed. And with that need is a responsibility to approach each other with respect and civility.

One day, many years ago, I received a call from John Houston; he wanted to talk about his daughter, Whitney, whose career he was managing. We agreed to meet at the Metropolitan Club, a private social club on the Upper East Side of Manhattan.

I was there at the designated time and waited and waited. He didn't seem like the sort of person who would be late. So I went outside, and there he was, waiting on

60th Street. He told me he thought he would be treated badly there because of his race. "They don't want me," he said.

"We're going in, and we're going to sit right in the middle," I told him, "and stay as long as we want to." We did, and nobody said bad things; nobody asked us to leave.

This was at the beginning of Whitney's career; she was about to skyrocket—what a voice! Her father came to me through the public relations firm, seeking help to get her reviewed. She wanted to be at Madison Square Garden; we found people who promoted acts and got her in. Her mother, Cissy, wanted to go, but all the seats were taken. We got her on a platform. A mother certainly should see her talented daughter perform at such a landmark venue. Later, a colleague and I were invited to Whitney's wedding.

Personal connections are everything. If you can make them and make them sincerely—that's the key word—you are doing right.

Oftentimes, people are very reluctant to reach out and form personal connections. Maybe they've never done that before. Maybe they're afraid of being turned down.

Where to begin? One approach that I have found successful is to make a list of people you would like to know in your field, the media, politics, or other realms. Then narrow that list to a manageable number. Do your research on backgrounds, such as where these people went to school, what boards they serve on, their charitable causes.

I know a fellow who wanted to reach three key people. He put their names in his electronic Rolodex, and when something would come up in the news related to their interests, he would contact them with the information. It was an enormous help in making connections.

Don't overdo it, of course. You want to be helpful, not pesky.

If your list is longer than ten people, it will be difficult to manage and overwhelming. Start with three; then, when you've made the connections, add three more, and keep building in that way.

As you read this, your reaction might be that you do not have enough time. There's only twenty-four hours in a day! But how you use those hours is up to you. Set your priorities.

Bob Strauss was a lawyer and a lobbyist in Washington who knew the power of connecting with people. He became so successful that all someone had to say was "I'm one of Bob Strauss's people," and doors would open for them on Capitol Hill.

Strauss founded a law firm and was steeped in politics, later representing his home state of Texas as chairman of the Democratic Party. In his long career, he advised three presidents—of both parties—and was appointed ambassador to the then–Soviet Union by President George H. W. Bush.

His success was rooted in being able to do something for others, and 100 percent of the time, he would look for you to do the same for him. For insight into the way he operated, consider his own words in an interview he did with the Association for Diplomatic Studies and Training.

I always dealt openly with the press, never misled them, never lied to them, always returned their phone calls. One time a very important columnist in this country said to me, "You know, Strauss, I called you last Wednesday, and you called me from your car Wednesday night on the way home at nine o'clock. I was already home, and you were in your car just going home and hadn't had supper yet, and you returned my phone call."

I said, "Well, that's why I returned it. I hadn't had time all day, and I didn't want to leave one of your calls unreturned."

He said, "You know, two days later I left the same call for so-and-so"—I don't recall his name—"and he hasn't returned it yet." Then he said to me, "And who do you think I'm going to screw in the next column, you or him?"[1]

Everyone comes to the table and asks, "How do I make myself known?" The answer is: don't try too hard. Others will make you memorable. Have other people talk about you.

One of my clients was a COO who wanted to become a CEO. My suggestion was to convince the board through advocates and contacts. This happened with a number of my clients, actually. Usually, after around six to nine months, we would reach the goal.

How was this done? By the way we positioned the individual: subtle yet noticeable. Here are steps you can take:

1. Think about your public profile: What has been written about you (is a new story needed?) or what you have written in the forms of op-eds, speeches, or professional papers. Write a book that demonstrates your expertise.
2. Understand who is making the decision and what motivates them. Find ways through their political parties, hospitals, art galleries, schools, or charities to support them and move forward.

3. Build a constituency within the company so that when you get the job, people will applaud you instead of asking, "Who's that?"

I encourage you to reach out in noncontroversial ways. Have dinners; have a discussion of ideas. Do this carefully and avoid offending anyone. You want your name out there so that a decision maker will snap their fingers and say, "That's the one!"

———

It can be extremely difficult breaking through institutions such as a statehouse, Congress, or the media. Every day, editors and reporters are besieged with hundreds of different requests; it's hard to get attention even if you have a great story. Congress is insulated. Getting to know so-and-so is difficult because you have to get through a number of people.

Everybody wants to get in the White House. But outside of a public tour, most people could just stand outside 1600 Pennsylvania Avenue and never get any closer.

But if you understand who's involved in certain topics or issues, such as nuclear power or fossil fuels, you can demonstrate how you can help them. Will the president ever see you? Probably not. But you'll be making personal connections with the power players.

A lot of times, clients think they have to get into the *New York Times* or the *Washington Post*. I say, let them come to you.

A client once said to me, "I've got to get into the *Wall Street Journal*." I replied, "Let me get you into twenty to thirty community papers, and it will add up over time."

If your story runs in, say, the *Detroit News* or the *Atlanta Journal-Constitution*, eventually it will be picked up by the Associated Press wire service and distributed to newspapers around the country and possibly the world.

Find a way to keep your name in front of people. And don't be shy about doing the same for your clients or company.

Don Hewitt, the original producer of *60 Minutes*, the longest-running, most-watched news magazine on television, came to lunch one day. He was a great guy and open to the notion of positioning clients' ideas, but I hadn't realized it. Later, he went back to his reporting staff, and they came up with segments, some of which were negative. It would have been very different if I had thought to pitch ideas of some good stories. Both broadcast and print are always looking for all sorts of different angles. One definition of a good newspaper is a mirror that reflects the community back to itself.

Pablo Picasso certainly wasn't shy about promoting himself. He said that anyone could be him, but what made him different was that he presented himself. Perhaps he was being uncharacteristically modest, as he created more than twenty thousand works of art, and almost everything he did changed the world—because he changed art.

Avoid equivocating; be firm and focused.

"Inspiration exists, but it has to find you working," Picasso said.

———

We had a client about a year ago who needed guidance through a difficult problem. A major educational institution was going to sanction him. We helped him avoid it. He remembered that and later called to hire us for an assignment at $40,000 a month. (You want to be sure, of course, that you do not compromise your integrity by advocating for someone criminal or sleazy.)

There is an art to making personal connections. Much depends on how you interact with others. Always be nice. Thank people for what they do. Know birthdays and send cards with a short personal note. Give credit to others.

Being connected is extremely important. It is worth your time and effort.

CHAPTER 4

The Power of Helping Others

J ohn H. Johnson, the founder and former CEO of the culture-defining *Ebony* and *Jet* magazines, knew the secret of the power of helping others. In his lifetime, he quietly assisted legions of others.

In this chapter, you, too, will learn this secret, as well as how to make your efforts most effective. Follow these directions, be inspired, and become a better person.

I knew Johnson from our Chicago days. He would sit in a barber chair in his office and discuss life with you. That sounds casual, which downplayed the fact that he was insightful and brilliant. With his leadership, his magazines became essential reads, chronicling important stories—for example, the civil rights movement.

Perhaps Johnson understood the power of helping others because of institutional obstacles early in life. Born in 1918 in Arkansas, his official education was truncated at eighth grade because no high schools for Black people existed in his town. He repeated eighth grade to keep learning. When his family moved to Chicago, he could finally attend high school and then college. In an arc of justice, Johnson would go on to receive at least thirty honorary university degrees and, among his many awards, the Presidential Medal of Freedom, the highest honor given to a civilian.

Johnson and I did many projects together for the Black community in Chicago, and—remarkably—he never took any credit.

You see, Johnson knew the secret: you help others not for personal recognition but for the altruism of creating a better community.

This is the power of helping others. You might consider this a personal obligation.

Now, here's a caveat. There always is one, isn't there?

Know who you are helping. By that I mean: do all you can to make sure your efforts are well placed. Before making financial donations to a cause, for example, research what percentage goes to administration or perks and how much actually ends up directed for services. There is little impact to just throwing your money to any cause. You want to make your contributions count as much as possible.

Trisha Bailey knew this. She wanted her contribution to her alma mater, the University of Connecticut, to relate to her experience as a member of the Huskies track team. In 2022, she donated the lead gift toward the $60 million renovation and expansion of the track field house where she had trained in the 1990s. She declined to disclose the amount of her gift, but it was the largest athletic donation in the university's long history.

Bailey lived in poverty as a child in Jamaica and with limited economic resources as a teenager in Hartford, Connecticut's capital city. Her time at UConn gave her the tools to become an entrepreneurial success in the medical-equipment industry and in real estate, with an eventual net worth of $650 million to $700 million.

"UConn gave me my first opportunity in life," Bailey remarked to *CT Insider.* "So for me, it's greater than simply a gift and bigger than a building in my name. It was the start of my life. They took a chance on the talent I didn't necessarily see, and they believed I would take advantage of the opportunities that were given me. And I have, with the blessings of God."[1]

She further explained her motives: "For me to give back so they can continue the tradition of supporting the kids on the field and off, it does something to my soul."[2]

As Bailey implies, you get back intrinsically when you give.

Find a cause that matches your interests and passions. Use your skills and talents to support it. Your help may not be monetary but rather the ability to help people think creatively. The same principle applies.

Once I knew a fellow who lost his top management job at a public utility. He called me for sixteen months straight, looking for advice. I helped him; one way was by positioning articles that put him in a favorable light.

Eventually, he was hired for a new top-ranking position. That should have been the happy ending, but it wasn't. He still held so much anger over losing his previous job that it spilled over into his management style within the new job. It didn't take long before he was fired again.

I had not sensed the depth of that personality trait. My investment was of time, which was lost, and a modicum of personal credibility, which could be regained. My lesson was to henceforth understand the nuances of how someone could use, and not abuse, my help.

Still, once you help someone, do not expect thanks, and don't call for it. That is unseemly and not the right thing to do.

Cathy Kangas figured out a creative way to help others—many others—in an authentic way that dovetailed with her interests and her company.

Through PRAI Beauty, her cruelty-free skincare company that is Leaping Bunny–certified, she donates a portion of sales to animal-rescue efforts globally.

That's not all. She also created the Cathy Kangas Foundation for Animals to save healthy animals from euthanasia in shelters. Every tax-deductible donation goes directly to help animals. In 2017, she created Free the Shelters, which sponsors free adoptions from shelters and within five years has saved more than eight thousand animals—and made thousands of owners and families happy.

Henry Timms came to New York knowing no one. He was the executive director of the 92nd Street Y for nearly a dozen years, where he made a name for himself—and enriched the community—by creating programs that fostered learning, civic responsibility, culture, and innovation. Now, as the president and CEO of the Lincoln Center for the Performing Arts, he wields enormous influence over the cultural life of New York City and beyond.

But Timms wanted to do even more, something of lasting value for the nonprofit world. From my Manhattan office, I would send him ideas now and then to consider and possibly flesh out. And so Timms created Giving Tuesday, an enormously successful annual event that encourages people to do good by raising money or volunteering time for a wide variety of nonprofits globally with thousands of partners.

Timms created Giving Tuesday for the good it could accomplish, not for any personal glory, though eventually he did receive meaningful awards.

Did he stop there? No. He cofounded the annual Social Good Summit, which opened the critical discussions held during United Nations Week to a wider audience and concurrent gatherings around the world.

Extending that idea, Timms partnered with Wesleyan University to develop an online course called "How to Change the World." The course description reads: "How can we use the things we share in common to address some of the most challenging problems facing the world? This course examines issues concerning poverty, the environment, technology, health care, gender, education, and activism to help us understand better how to initiate positive change."

In the first year, 51,000 people participated. The course is *free*.

As Robert Kennedy famously said, "One person can make a difference, and everyone should try."

————

What any single individual does still counts a great deal—more so than most imagine. Because community service is needed today more than ever, each of us should ask: What am I personally doing to help? No person is an island unto themself. We are all part of the human family. Yes, there is a certain nobility in helping the needy—doing the right thing, as it were—but also, one must never forget that there, but for the grace of God, go I.

Father Ted Hesburgh, president of Notre Dame University for thirty-five years, would befriend the CEO and the lowest person alike. He was that kind of guy. Yet he was quite powerful himself. He made Notre Dame, my alma mater, one of the most influential Catholic universities in the country, and on the national stage, he was notable for his stance against the Vietnam War and his work on the US Civil Rights Commission.

Twice when I was in the chapel, he came and knelt next to me. He motivated people by his beliefs and took people to the next level.

I'll never forget what he said to me after a meeting he'd had with the NCAA over the university's football program. He told me that he got what he wanted but left a little bit. "Make them feel like they won something," he said. That was a valuable lesson.

Today, not only are we alerted to others' needs almost instantly, but we also have the ability to connect and provide services in ways and on a time line never before possible.

In a wonderful circle of reciprocity, the more you truly try to improve society for the common good, the better of a person you will become and the more you will experience a sense of fulfillment.

It is in your hands to make a better world for all who live in it.

———

Nelson Mandela

CHAPTER 5

Social Media:
Make It Work for You

D o you need to understand social media? You bet you do.

I cannot think of anyone out there who does not know about social media or who is not attracted by it. Corporations are seeing what it can deliver for business—both positive and negative.

So you need to get involved here. Knowing what social media can do for you—or how it might be used against you—is very important.

Jennifer Sey was in line to become the next CEO of Levi Strauss & Co., a firm so well branded that its name is synonymous with one of its leading products, denim jeans. A twenty-year employee, she was the chief marketing officer before her promotion to global brand president in October 2020, making her the first woman in that position. Profits more than doubled under her leadership, she said. Just a year later, she was being vetted for CEO. But then, suddenly, she quit. And she rejected a $1 million settlement.

What went wrong?

Twitter and COVID-19. Her boss told her that her Twitter presence was "too problematic for [her] to hold this role of CEO" and that there was no "viable path forward for [her] at this company,"[1] Sey told a *New York Times* reporter in a March 2022 story appropriately titled "She Was a Candidate to Lead Levi's. Then She Started Tweeting."

Her tweets were critical of school closings during the early months of the COVID-19 pandemic. After she moved her two young children from San Francisco to Denver, where schools were open—and explained why in tweets—she was invited to appear on Laura Ingraham's Fox News show, which gave even greater exposure to her anti–COVID-19 closing views. Some Levi's employees complained.

"While they didn't try to muzzle me outright," Sey said of Levi's management, "I was told repeatedly to 'think about what I was saying.'"[2]

With two sides to every issue, you can expect that there are differing interpretations of why the company's rising star was suddenly out the door. Sey turned down the hefty severance package, believing the nondisclosure agreement would have prevented her from talking about the matter. The whole issue comes down to free speech, she maintains. But it appears the company found her vocal positions about school closings and public-health guidelines problematic when it was trying to set pandemic policies to keep employees and consumers safe.

Social media is a powerful tool; however, the downside is that it blurs the line between a public persona and a private life. These are difficult, if not impossible, to separate now.

Must you shun social media for the sake of your career? Absolutely not. But you must know how to use it wisely and understand your position as well as that of your company's before you post for all the world to see.

———

"The fact is that it's impossible to separate the personal use of social from the professional, and everything you say online can and will be used against you. There are ways in which you can try to safeguard your privacy and control who sees particular content, but the onus is on you to be vigilant. So, the more seriously you can take your social-media activities, the better."[3] That's sage advice from Sreenath "Sree" Sreenivasan, a former chief digital officer for noteworthy places such as the Metropolitan Museum of Art, Columbia University, and the City of New York. In 2016, he was named the most influential online chief digital officer by the CDO Club.

I first met Sreenivasan when he was the dean of students at Columbia University's Graduate School of Journalism in the early 2000s; he had helped create the New Media program at Columbia in 1994.

"When I discovered new media and internet, it was to me a moment like seeing color television for the first time. I remember that excitement," he said in an interview for my 2007 book, *Power and Influence: The Rules Have Changed*. "And I saw this as something that was going to change our lives."

They certainly shaped his professional life. With various high-placed appointments and multiple awards, he became the CEO and cofounder of Digimentors, a digital- and virtual-events consulting company. During the COVID-19 pandemic, he hosted multiple shows and interviewed hundreds of experts in an effort to disseminate accurate information about the global crisis. In 2022, he became the managing director of CronkitePro, a new professional-education and skills-training initiative at Arizona State University's Walter Cronkite School of Journalism and Mass Communication.

"Social media was once mostly just for fun, but not anymore," Sreenivasan notes in his *New York Times* guide to using social media in one's career. "Social media is now a critical part of the way people in most walks of life communicate and a key part of how work gets done—from corporations to government."[4]

Katie Delahaye Paine, a public relations and social media measurement expert, puts it simply: "If they're not talking about you on social media, you don't exist."[5]

"Social media" is a broad term. It includes social networks, such as Facebook, Twitter, Snapchat, and Instagram; media-sharing networks, such as TikTok and YouTube; and professional groups, such as LinkedIn. There are discussion groups such as Reddit, rating sites such as Yelp. The ever-growing roster goes on and on.

Don't try to master them all; you will spread yourself too thin. Explore what fits best with your goals. For example, be on LinkedIn for personal contacts and Facebook (now under the parent company Meta) and/or Twitter for personal and corporate branding. But be on the lookout for new platforms that may have a more optimal reach to your customers, clients, and potential new ones. Be aware when one platform is getting a reputation for stodginess or, conversely, unchecked controversy or conspiracies.

Social media is always changing, so "it's important to keep up with the evolution of the platforms and to keep looking for ways to optimize your use of the available tools,"[6] Sreenivasan advises.

An attractive idea can get traction through social media. The whole goal is to figure out your, your client's, or your company's objective in using that particular social-media platform.

Facebook has evolved from a method for families and classmates to stay in touch—posting milestones or pictures of lunch—to a way for companies and nonprofits to make pitches that can be shared and seen by massive numbers. It connects you with influencers in your field and builds your brand through sharing informative or interesting articles. If you have written a published piece—for example, an op-ed—then Facebook is an effective tool for getting more people to see it.

Some users prefer to maintain separate accounts for the personal, with privacy controls, and the professional. But, again, that doesn't mean that what you say in your personal account cannot seep over to influence your professional life.

Twitter, once used more by government and business leaders and journalists, is also useful for drawing attention to your articles, as you can tweet links with a compelling hook and hashtags. And the benefits from building a network of followers are real. One way to do this is to have something to say. That sounds obvious, but just retweeting other people doesn't draw attention to yourself or prompt others to follow you. Retweet with a relevant comment. Establish yourself as knowledgeable in your field. And notice what others are saying. But be alert to what is opinion purported as fact.

Remember how I mentioned in this book's introduction that everything is changing at a rapid pace? As I write, Twitter is drastically changing. The online platform has been a lightning rod for criticism for either letting misinformation go unchallenged or, on the other hand, kicking off some users, most notably former president Donald Trump.

"After close review of recent Tweets from the @realDonaldTrump account and the context around them—specifically how they are being received and interpreted on and off Twitter—we have permanently suspended the account due to the risk of further incitement of violence,"[7] Twitter explained in a blog post on January 8, 2021, two days after the insurrection at the Capitol.

Elon Musk, the world's wealthiest person, started a process to buy Twitter in April 2022 and by October 27 of that year—after starts and stops—completed the $44 billion acquisition. In fewer than two weeks, he laid off 3,700 employees, roughly half the workforce, and began charging users to receive the coveted blue check mark that signifies a verified account. This unleashed some chaos; the pay-for-a-blue-check process was put on hold. Many were watching closely to see whether previously suspended users will be allowed to return, and in late 2022, Musk reinstated Donald Trump's Twitter account.

Enter a Twitter alternative, Mastodon.

The CEO of the decentralized microblogging site Mastodon, Eugen Rochko, told CNN and *TIME* that the site attracted 120,000 new users in just four days after Musk bought Twitter, pushing the social network to one million active users and reportedly 4.5 million accounts.

Rochko said he started Mastodon because he didn't trust Twitter's "top-down control." Instead, the crowd-funded site operates on server groups of interest with users empowered to monitor hateful content by, in essence, shunning it. "I guess you could call it the democratic process,"[8] Rochko said.

As powerful as social media may be, it's not always the answer.

A client came to me the other day and wanted to get a big project moving—he wanted social media. I said, "There are seven people you need to reach, including one in government and one in media. Get your argument in front of those seven people. They are the ones who count for this project." He did not use social media. Instead, he found unique ways to reach out to each of the seven. He was successful.

How do you know the best way to get your idea or project moving? I tell clients to first grab a blank sheet of paper. In two to three sentences, write what you want to do. Some people would rather turn it over to staff to come up with a fifty-page report, but you have to be able to distill it down to its essence before you can pitch it to others. You need to figure out who the decision makers are and decide on the most productive way to reach them. And social media won't always be the best way.

There is a proper and useful place for social media, of course. Sreenivasan points to several significant benefits. Those who watch sites closely and monitor posts can spot trends and maybe even discover ideas they can apply. Social media can help you connect with contacts in a more meaningful and personal way and allow you to develop new ones. On another level, it can spotlight your work and company and enhance your professional and corporate brand.

———

The line between personal and professional life cannot be clearly drawn with a Sharpie.

The First Amendment protects freedom of speech, but keep in mind that this freedom is from government interference. The amendment begins with "Congress shall make no law." Court cases have expanded the definition of speech to include expression, such as the wearing of flags or the carrying of signs. Corporations can, and should, set their own policies regarding social media. I cannot overemphasize the importance of having your own defined position and knowing your company's policies.

Social media cannot be ignored; it will get even more impactful as we go forward. It's a powerful tool. Know how to use it—and make it work for you.

CHAPTER 6

You Can Be a Great Communicator in Every Way

You have a choice.

    You can be a great communicator. Or you can ignore outreach.

This chapter tells you how to be a great communicator. Make that your choice.

Effective communication is *the* essential skill for achieving and maintaining power and influence. You might have the best ideas in the industry, but if you can't communicate them, you'll go nowhere.

Communication skills were the number-one "soft skill" that job postings on ZipRecruiter (6.1 million of them) listed as a requirement between 2021 and 2022, the employment firm noted in its 2022 Job Market Outlook for Grads report.[1]

This chapter will cover how to be skillful in the many aspects of communication—from how to write and deliver presentations; talk at meetings; relay your message to employees, clients, and investors; understand and use body language; and harness communication to build business relationships.

Rhonda, a vice president of sales at a national electronics company, is about to deliver a crucial speech. She's put a lot of effort into writing and polishing it and has rehearsed with a handful of trusted peers, who all liked her presentation. She feels confident as she walks to the podium at the firm-wide sales meeting called to introduce new products and set high goals. Standing straight and tall, yet appearing relaxed, she pauses for a moment to look at the audience and increase their anticipation. She begins relating a story from her days as a field rep, like many in the audience. She segues to a colorful slideshow presentation illustrating her positive assessment of the company's sales outlook for the year. Her gestures and facial expressions are animated, punctuated, perfect.

As her speech comes to a close, Rhonda walks to the edge of the stage, scans the crowd, and challenges the audience to gain entry into the company's annual winners' circle. But the enthusiasm that should be generated isn't there. She finds herself stunned.

Rhonda apparently checked off all the boxes for doing and saying the right things, but her presentation didn't click. What went wrong?

Keep reading, and I will tell you.

Nick Morgan, a public-speaking coach and author, tells the tale of the executive I've called Rhonda in "How to Become an Authentic Speaker," published in the *Harvard Business Review*.[2] The answer to why Rhonda's presentation fell flat isn't necessarily obvious.

As Deborah Tannen, the linguistic expert and author, says, "Communication isn't as simple as saying what you mean."[3] Effective communication stems from *how* you convey your message, how you make it memorable, and, importantly, how you listen.

Many managers believe communication is just about how you say your message. But communication is neither style nor the eloquence of your speech. It is solid thinking translated into clear messages. Communication is the very heart of management. It is critical if you want to be successful.

Phil Smith of Marathon Oil understood the power of words. He would select each word very carefully, and each word would carry meaning, the way in poetry every word must count.

You never left his office without feeling something positive. Was he perfectly coiffed and sporting gold cuff links? No. He was bald and would stop at the corner store on his way to work for coffee and the paper, not expecting anyone to get either for him.

Am I talking about the head of Marathon Oil? Not so. Smith was a member of the communication department;

he never wanted to be head of the company. But he wanted to see the fullness and treatment of his ideas. He controlled ideas. People came to him—he had influence.

As Smith did, you must remember to choose your words carefully, whether written or spoken. You have to keep your overall level of communication up to your highest standards. This includes even a quick email. Your email needs to be well composed. An email containing spelling errors or poor grammar undermines the message and knocks the sender down a notch or two.

And you must focus your communication. The more focused your communication is, the deeper the impression it will make. Focus begins with clear thinking.

Ask yourself what result or action you want before you send the email, pick up the phone, speak up at the meeting, or write the speech—even if that result is simply a favorable impression. Make sure your tone and word choice match your goal. Be succinct. Always. No one wants or has the time to wade through verbiage.

Importantly, focus on the needs and interests of the person or organization with whom you are communicating. For example, when speaking one-on-one, use active listening. Instead of thinking about how you can sound smart or what you'll say next, really listen to what the other person is saying. Show interest through body language, such as leaning forward slightly and making eye contact, and by asking relevant questions. Use active listening in a range of situations, such as networking or a meeting about an employee's concerns.

Jack Welch, the former CEO of General Electric, was a master of active listening. He could sit on a park bench and have conversations about, say, the Red Sox or Yankees with anyone and give them his full attention. Most CEOs won't do that; they want only lofty talk. Incidentally, in the conference room, Welch's skill came in handy for drawing out novel ideas.

Let me give you an example of poor communication. A few years ago, I was consulting for a CEO who was about to take his company public. (I will not embarrass him by using his name.) I advised him to tailor his message to investors with solid information on why his company's stock could benefit them. But he didn't listen. He said, "Yeah, I don't really have time for this." He was wrong. The enthusiasm wasn't there, the public offering did not reach goals, and before long, he was out of a job.

You see, he was operating from *his* perspective, not considering what others needed or wanted to hear.

Frank Luntz, a top international communications consultant, puts it this way: it's not what you say; it's what people hear.[4]

Luntz came up with "Words to Use" and "Words to Lose" for a project with an energy company in Hawaii. After research and polls, he determined that the public cared more about the future of their children than other factors such as safety or cost. So for the company's communication, he advised that instead of "impact on society," it should say "impact on kids/future generations." Instead of "a smart, intelligent approach," it should say "a responsible approach"; instead of "the consequences of delay," the "benefits of acting now."

You get the idea. There's nothing inherently wrong with "a smart, intelligent approach"—it just wasn't a message that would appeal to the target audience.

Know your audience, whether it's one person or an entire state or country. Make your message resonate.

Avoid clichés. Sometimes I'll make my point to clients by saying, "Avoid clichés like the plague."

Clichés are overworn phrases that have been used so many times, they have lost meaning. They now signify laziness in speaking. Instead of saying something original, the speaker resorts to the easy-to-reach phrase.

Some examples overused in business: "at the end of the day," "win-win," "get the ball rolling," "think outside the box," "back to the drawing board," "let's touch base," "move the goal post." (Notice the preponderance of sports references!)

Don't be a lazy speaker; be original.

And for leaders, in particular, be clear.

"Leaders frequently espouse dozens of cliché-infused declarations such as 'Let's focus on the key priorities this quarter,' 'Customers come first,' or 'We need a full-court press in engineering this month,'" writes John Hamm in a *Harvard Business Review* essay. "Over and over again, they present grand, overarching—yet fuzzy—notions of where they think the company is going. Too often, they assume everyone shares the same definitions of broad terms like vision, loyalty, accountability, customer relationships, teamwork, focus, priority, culture, frugality, decision making, results, and so on."[5]

The problem is, these leaders are not understood by senior managers who refrain from asking for clarification for fear of seeming not smart, so they in turn pass the vague marching orders to their staff, who are left to their own interpretations.

"Leaders simply assume that the exact meaning of their words is obvious; they're surprised to learn not only that their message has been unclear but that their teams crave definitions so they aren't forced to guess what the boss has in mind,"[6] Hamm found in his research.

Think about the ramifications.

A CEO who communicates precisely to ten direct reports, who then each communicate with equal precision to forty more staff, will successfully align the vision with clear goals within the organization. Guessing or misinterpreting are replaced by clarity and direction.

Aside from eschewing clichés, whether in writing or speaking, always use the active voice, never the passive. Make your sentences energetic, not flabby. Make your argument as short as you can—pages and pages bore the pants off people, and your audience will be offended if you can't boil it down.

Engage with your relevant life experiences; people will relate. Use storytelling techniques versus teaching.

Former Hewlett-Packard CEO Meg Whitman learned the value of storytelling the hard way.

She spent $144 million of her own money on her 2010 campaign to become governor of California. She lost to Democrat Jerry Brown, and, upon reflection, she said it taught her to be a better communicator. You would think she would've already been an effective communicator; before Hewlett-Packard, she was the CEO of eBay, shepherding the three-year-old start-up with thirty employees and under $5 million in revenues to fifteen thousand employees and $8 billion in sales, plus locations in thirty countries, a decade later. She was considered at both eBay and Hewlett-Packard to be a focused and optimistic leader. In the Biden administration, she was nominated to be the ambassador to Kenya and was approved by the Senate in 2022.

"What I learned was it's not the facts and figures," Whitman said in an interview with CNBC. "It's not the left brain. It is the stories you tell to communicate the vision that you're trying to get the organization to rally around."[7]

Stories are remembered twenty-two times more than mere information and facts, according to professor Jennifer Aaker, a behavioral scientist at the Stanford University Graduate School of Business. One of her focuses is the power of story in decision-making, as well as transmitting ideas through social networks.

Though you should relate with your true experiences, remember that the story you tell is not about you. It's about the person you helped, the problem you solved, the lesson learned. No need to overcomplicate—keep it to one takeaway per story.

For business purposes, the structure of a powerful story has four primary parts, as Matthew Pollard outlines in his book *The Introvert's Edge to Networking*.

1. The problem, want, or need. Spend about 35 percent of your story here. Connect emotionally so your audience will want to hear the outcome.

2. Analysis and implementation. Share the realization made and use collaborative language (not "I did this"; rather, "As we implemented stage one together . . ."). This section should be no more than 20 percent of your story.

3. The outcome. This is where you recap the costs saved or trouble avoided. Emphasize the emotional benefits. Focus about 35 percent of your story on this section.

4. Moral/high-level learning. Never let your listeners draw their own conclusions, even if you think they are obvious. Spell it out. This is the last 10 percent of your story.

Storytelling devices work in conversations or presentations—not necessarily in meetings, where your contributions must be succinct. In such situations, as always, pay close attention to your language. "I think . . ." sounds weak. "I'm sorry, but . . ." is even weaker. Never begin with an apology for participating! Avoid touchy-feely words if you want to be taken seriously.

Linguistic styles can differ between men and women, Tannen notes based upon her research. "Women tend to say *I'm sorry* more frequently than men, and often they intend it in this way—as a ritualized means of expressing concern," Tannen explains. "It's one of the many learned elements of conversational style that girls often use to establish rapport. Ritual apologies—like other conversational rituals—work well when both parties share the same assumptions about their use. But people who utter frequent ritual apologies may end up appearing weaker, less confident, and literally more blameworthy than people who don't."[8]

Keep in mind that besides possible gender differences, there may be cultural differences in how language is used and interpreted. It is vitally important to be aware of these interpretations as workplaces strive, appropriately, to become more diverse and inclusive.

When speaking, as in writing, use active, muscular verbs. And please, avoid the temptation to "-ize" a word. Don't promise to "prioritize"; say that you will "set priorities." Use the strong language of success.

———

Let's get back to Rhonda and her flop of a presentation. It would seem she did everything right—made eye contact, used hand gestures, displayed colorful PowerPoint slides, told a story, moved around the stage—so what went wrong?

"If asked about these speeches, we might describe them as 'calculated,' 'insincere,' 'not real,' or 'phoned in.' We probably wouldn't be able to say exactly why the performance wasn't compelling. The speaker just didn't seem *authentic*," Morgan notes. "Authenticity—including the ability to communicate authentically with others—has become an important leadership attribute. When leaders have it, they can inspire their followers to make extraordinary efforts on behalf of their organizations. When they don't, cynicism prevails and few employees do more than the minimum necessary to get by."[9]

This issue of authenticity is quite complicated. It's about the way our brains perceive and process information. "If your spoken message and your body language are mismatched, audiences will respond to the nonverbal message every time. Gestures speak louder than words," Morgan says. "Gesture precedes conscious thought and thought precedes words—even if by no more than a tiny fraction of a second . . . speakers end up employing those gestures at the same time that—or even slightly after—they speak the associated words. Although audiences are not consciously aware of this unnatural sequence, their innate ability to read body language leads them to feel that something's wrong—that the speaker is inauthentic."[10]

So is it better to avoid rehearsing your presentation or speech and just wing it? Absolutely not! But you don't need to rehearse your body language. Instead, Morgan advises, work around four goals:

1. Being open with your audience
2. Connecting with your audience
3. Being passionate about your topic
4. Listening to your audience

"If you are able to sincerely realize these feelings, your body language will take care of itself, emerging naturally and at the right moment,"[11] Morgan says. And, as a result, your listeners will know you're the real thing.

Keeping with the science of communication a moment longer, consider Albert Mehrabian's classic 7-38-55 communication model. Mehrabian, a psychology professor at the University of California, Los Angeles, introduced the concept in his 1971 book *Silent Messages*.

Not a catchy name for a communication model, perhaps, but the point is that when we speak, 7 percent of all the meaning, feelings, and attitudes we try to communicate comes through the words we use—only

7 percent!—while 38 percent comes through our tone and voice, and the remaining whopping 55 percent comes through body language.

It will do you well to pay attention to what your body is communicating—from the way you sit, stand, listen, speak—and make sure the message is consistent with your words.

Let's take a few moments to focus on the fascinating topic of body language. You need to know how to communicate the right nonverbal message and, on the flip side, how to interpret the signals others are sending. With first impressions made in a matter of seconds, the way you present yourself has impact even before you say your first word.

"Slow down your breathing, pull your shoulders back and down, stand up straight and firmly plant your feet on the ground," advises Amy Cuddy, the author of *Presence* whose TED Talk on body language has been viewed more than 65 million times. "If you're carrying yourself in a way that's powerful and proud, you're saying to yourself, 'I'm safe. I'm OK. I deserve to be here.' And that is what comes across."[12] This helps establish trustworthiness.

I'd like to share with you these five tips I came up with and first delineated in a Dilenschneider Group Red Book for clients.

1. **Face people directly.** Even a quarter turn away creates a barrier (the "cold shoulder"), signaling a lack of interest and causing the other person to shut down. Physical obstructions are especially detrimental to the effective exchange of ideas. Take away anything that blocks your view or forms a barrier between you and the rest of the team. Close your laptop, turn off your cell phone, put your purse or briefcase to the side.

2. **Maintain positive eye contact.** Looking at someone's eyes transmits energy and indicates interest. As long as you're looking at me, I believe that I have your full attention. Eye contact is most effective when both parties feel its intensity is appropriate for the situation. This may differ with introverts/extroverts, men/women, or between people of different cultures, but in general, greater eye contact—especially in intervals lasting four to five seconds—almost always leads to a greater level of approval.

3. **Use open gestures.** Keeping your movements relaxed, using open arm gestures, and showing the palms of your hands are all silent signals of credibility and candor. Individuals with open gestures are perceived more positively and are

more persuasive than those with closed gestures (arms crossed or hands hidden or held close to the body).

4. **Use your head.** The next time you are in a conversation where you're trying to encourage the other person to speak more, nod your head using clusters of three nods at regular intervals. Research shows that people will talk three to four times more than usual when the listener nods in this manner. You'll be amazed at how this single nonverbal signal can trigger such a positive response.

5. **Activate your smile power.** The human brain prefers happy faces, recognizing them more quickly than those with negative expressions. Most important, smiling directly influences how other people respond to you. When you smile at someone, they will almost always smile in return. And, because facial expressions trigger corresponding feelings (a reaction called "facial feedback"), the smile you get back will actually change that person's emotional state in a positive way. This one simple act will instantly and powerfully send a message of warmth and welcome.

Remember that team members will be watching you *all* the time, and they'll be waiting to see if your behavior is congruent in both formal and informal settings. When one CEO hosted a corporate function designed to gather ideas from participants, he sent all the right nonverbal signals during the presentations, nodding, smiling, etc.—but spent the breaks sitting far away from the group, reading a newspaper. It was only natural shyness that caused him to withdraw, but by now I'm sure you can accurately guess how the other people in his group evaluated his behavior.

———

Communication doesn't end with your presentation, proposal, or interview. You must use communication thoughtfully to solidify and nurture your network of relationships and build your brand.

How to do this? One way is through a carefully written op-ed—an argument of persuasion that could appear in a newspaper, magazine, or online site. This would build your credibility and influence. The key is not to pontificate but rather to persuade. You would be smart to look back at the Founding Fathers and how they expressed their views. Benjamin Franklin, Alexander Hamilton,

Patrick Henry—they all had very specific styles that recommend them.

Write about what you know, something related to your expertise. And remember what I said earlier about active, muscular language and clarity.

When your piece is published, send links to your list with a short note ("I think it will be worth your time . . ." or "I'd like to know what you think . . ."). You are establishing yourself as an expert and finding a friendly, helpful way to keep your name in front of your contacts.

Email and texting are the go-to methods of communication these days. But the same rules apply—always use correct grammar and spelling (it takes just a minute to double-check), be brief, and be clear. Your recipient shouldn't have to read halfway through your email to figure out what you're talking about. As tempting as it is, avoid using emojis to express your thoughts unless you're communicating with your children. You might see an emoji as playful, but it's not a professional way to communicate in the corporate world.

When you receive an email, make it a point to reply within twenty-four hours. You might not have the answer that soon, so say so and convey that you will respond fully when you do have it.

I'm sure that, like me, you've sent emails and then are left to wonder whether the recipient ever got it or read it—or if it just went through a spam filter. Respond promptly. Not only is this courteous but also it reinforces that you are reliable.

Now, a little time management is necessary here; otherwise, you'll be tethered to your inbox all day. Set aside a particular time every day to address your emails, unless one comes through that is a true emergency requiring an immediate response.

On a more individual note, embrace the intrinsic value of the personal touch. In our nonstop, sometimes frantic lives, we may easily forget the importance of gratitude, the value of that often brief but vital connection we make when we take a moment to smile and say "thank you." People benefit from saying it as much as the one listening appreciates hearing it. Vast emotional distances may be overcome in a moment by a "thank you" that conveys "I value you and what you do."

Here's a suggestion from experts about the art of saying "thank you": smile and make eye contact. Nothing says "insincerity" more than a mumbled thank-you from someone who doesn't even bother to look you in the eye.

But don't overdo it. Gushing makes nearly everyone uncomfortable. Acknowledge specifically what someone did for you, but don't go into your life story. Be grateful, be pleasant, and be brief. Above all else, be sincere.

For a gift, a meal, or any other extraordinary act of kindness, write a thank-you note. Yes, I said *write*. In our email-driven culture, a written note is special. It should be prompt, it should be personal, and it should mention the act that inspired the thank-you and what it meant to you. It should never, ever be perfunctory.

And do it yourself. Do not delegate sending a note of thanks to someone else. It means something special only if it comes from you. Many CEOs have a box of personalized cards at the ready so they can let others know of their gratitude promptly. On the other hand, resist an abominable new development: fill-in-the-blank thank-yous.

It is my belief that today's well-motivated executive who has built their team wisely does not hesitate to show appreciation to colleagues, subordinates, friends, relatives, and business associates. Today's successful leaders know that saying "thank you" is not a sign of weakness or insecurity but an expression of personal confidence.

Communication takes many forms. Understand and employ the various methods, tools, and psychology to become an effective communicator. In time, you can personify the art of communication.

CHAPTER 7

The Right Way to
Make Your Mistakes

**Anyone who has never made a mistake
has never tried anything new.**

Albert Einstein

N o one wants to make mistakes. Mistakes are embarrassing. They can be costly. The consequences can be great. Worst, mistakes prove we're not perfect, right? Well, no one is perfect, no matter your level of responsibilities, the empire you have built, or your financial worth.

Mistakes will happen if you are taking risks, as I suggest.

Now, keep in mind I'm talking about career risks. Not "mistakes" that are obviously poor judgment, such as driving after a few drinks. No excuses there.

But in business-driven decisions that turn out to be mistakes, there's a right way to handle the ensuing situations.

In management (and life), you've got to own up to your mistakes. Never try to blame someone else, even if it's not entirely your fault.

One of the most talented architects I've ever met exemplifies the virtue.

I was in the room at the Ritz Paris when I. M. Pei was pitching his idea for a novel treatment of a beloved public institution in the City of Light. At the time, I represented his company, I. M. Pei & Partners. Hearing the pitch was France's president, François Mitterrand, and the mayor of Paris, Jacques Chirac.

"Absolutely no way," Mitterrand dug in. "There is no way the French people will stand for it!"

Chirac disagreed. "The French people are always avant-garde," he insisted. "They will embrace it."

Would Pei's unusual design fly? Outwardly, he seemed serene, but this was his professional challenge of a lifetime.

Pei's reputation for innovation was well known—he had designed the L'Enfant Plaza in Washington, DC, the JFK Library in Boston, and the Rock and Roll Hall of Fame in Cleveland, among many, many projects—but go back a few years to see why it was uncertain his idea would be endorsed.

Along with the multiple high-profile projects and numerous awards, his career had experienced a major setback: the John Hancock Tower. It was a sixty-story structure that was to house offices for John Hancock Insurance at Copley Square in Boston's Back Bay. The entire city loved it, but problems developed, such as sinkholes. But that was not the worst of it.

I'll never forget this scene. We were conducting a news tour of the new building, with the stunning glass facade designed to reflect the city skyline, when on the top floor, all of a sudden, two windows popped out. The wind was intense; some people hid under desks. It was frightening. And embarrassing for the architects.

This was extremely dangerous—the windows weighed five hundred pounds each, and you can imagine the impact below from dozens of stories up high. The building swayed in the high winds off the bay, and more windows fell out.

After much analysis, the problem was found to be in the insulating glass. I won't get into the science of it, but the result was a $75 million project (in the early 1970s) that ballooned to $175 million and took an extra five years for completion as every pane of glass—10,348 of them—was replaced.

Pei himself had not designed the tower nor specified the glass. The designer was Henry Cobb. But Pei's name was on the firm, and the firm's name was on the plans. So he took responsibility.

With humility and perseverance, we move forward and improve.

The presentation in Paris I witnessed was for—maybe you've guessed it—a new entrance to the Musée de Louvre. Chirac won that day at the Ritz, and the modernist pyramid of glass—yes, glass!—opened to great acclaim in 1989; the French people did indeed embrace it, as did visitors from all over. It became a must-see in Paris. The Louvre is one of the most frequented museums in the world, with nearly ten million people visiting in 2019 before the pandemic. The glass pyramid, a doorway to the famous artwork inside the museum, is itself a work of art.

The year after his glass-pyramid entrance opened, Pei, who came to the United States from China at the age of eighteen, retired. Two years later, he was awarded the US Presidential Medal of Freedom.

Pei had integrity, the kind that engenders respect.

People make mistakes; however, the biggest mistake is failing to learn from them.

Once, I wrote a piece that I thought was terrific. I brought it to my boss at Hill+Knowlton, Ed Doherty, a tough, crusty Irishman who was very good at what he did. I sat in front of his desk and waited for the cascade of compliments I was sure would come.

Doherty looked over his glasses at me. "This is really terrible."

And then, for the next four hours, he went over the piece line by line and showed me where I split infinitives or used passive verbs. It was one of the best educations of my life.

Remember what playwright George Bernard Shaw once admonished: "Success does not consist in never making mistakes but in never making the same one a second time."

To extract the most learning from your mistakes, first consider how you talk to yourself about them. Do you wallow in self-recriminations? Do you amplify the negativity? That can be self-defeating and make you too cautious to stretch again.

Henry Ford memorably expressed it this way: "The man who thinks he can and the man who thinks he can't are both right."

Oprah Winfrey was once "down there in the hole," as she puts it. After she started OWN, the Oprah Winfrey Network, in 2011, ratings, well, stunk—and she was losing money.

"Now when you're down there in the hole, it looks like failure," she said in her commencement speech at Harvard University in 2013. "When that moment comes, it's really okay to feel bad for a little while. Give yourself time to mourn what you think you may have lost—but then, here's the key: learn from every mistake because every experience, encounter, and particularly your mistakes are there to teach you and force you into being more who you are."[1]

Within a year, the basic cable network was profitable.

When it comes to your mistakes, look realistically at what went wrong. Could it have been anticipated? Could it have been prevented? What could you or your team or your company have done differently?

Sometimes from this sort of clear-eyed examination comes the kernel of another idea. The original idea may have failed, but from it can spring something even better.

Behavioral studies have shown that learning from getting something wrong is stronger than from having the right answer in the first place. Think back to your classroom days. If you were called upon and got an answer wrong, you were embarrassed, most likely, but then would pay sharper attention to the correct answer. You would remember it in a way that you might not have otherwise.

Staff will watch how you handle a mistake. If you ignore it, your staff won't say anything but will harbor the view that you won't come to grips with it. I've had many top executives tell me they're not going to talk about a mistake, and I always tell them it will hurt them, and their company, to not speak out.

By owning up and handling a situation with humility, energy, and positivity, you are setting the best example for your company or organization.

Not only will you gain respect, as Pei did, but you will also send the message that employees can feel safe in admitting to mistakes while striving and find constructive ways to move forward.

JPMorgan Chase CEO Jamie Dimon extracted this lesson from one of the worst losses of the company. A decade ago, trades by a London-based employee led to a whopping loss of more than $5 billion. Yes, *billion*.

In a letter to shareholders, Dimon admitted it was "the stupidest and most embarrassing situation [he had] ever been a part of."[2] But it taught him to ask the hard questions of employees without fear of hostility or friction.

"Confronting people when necessary or asking hard questions is not an insult," he wrote. "It doesn't mean you lack collegiality or don't trust the individual. In fact, asking hard questions is what we owe one another to protect ourselves from mistakes and self-inflicted wounds."[3]

Instead of appearing confrontational, this approach can help employees feel protected. They can trust that their CEO will not let poor decisions—which affect everyone—go unchallenged.

If there are absolutely no mistakes in a company, then no one is taking a risk, and innovation will atrophy. You know the eventual result for that company.

Perfection is a fallacy. Do not seek perfection in yourself because that will eventually stifle your risk-taking and lead to some restless nights. On the flip side, if you already think you're always right—well, you're wrong. And you close yourself off from good ideas and discourage employees from suggesting them.

Amazon founder Jeff Bezos had several failed ideas, and expensive ones at that. For example, an online auction site, zShops, fizzled. Ever heard of Amazon's Fire smartphone? Probably not. Within months of launching in 2014, the price of the phone went from $199 to ninety-nine cents, and the company took a quarterly loss of $170 million.

"If you think that's a big failure, we're working on much bigger failures right now. And I am not kidding," Bezos told the *Washington Post*. "Some of them are going to make the Fire Phone look like a tiny little blip."[4]

What Bezos told shareholders is this: "Failure and invention are inseparable twins."[5]

In 2021, Bezos stepped down as CEO of Amazon and became its executive chair. He is, of course, one of the top five wealthiest people in the world (as of 2022).

With calculated risk-taking, you also need perseverance.

The brand Dyson is now synonymous with high-end, efficient vacuum cleaners. But it took James Dyson 5,127 prototypes—5,127!—over the course of fifteen years before he had a suitable product to pitch to retailers in England. None took the bite. So he launched it through catalogues in Japan, where it became a quick success, and soon he had enough income to open his own facility. The firm now also makes commercial hand dryers, bladeless fans, and air purifiers.

Good thing James Dyson believed in what he was attempting, persevered, and didn't stop at prototype number 5,126.

I was at the airport in Indianapolis some decades ago when I happened to meet Dr. Robert Cade. We chatted about what he had helped develop at the University of Florida, a sports drink called Gatorade.

"I've got to take you to my client," I told him. At first Cade demurred, saying Gatorade was for football players, but he later agreed.

We canceled our flights and went straight to Stokely-Van Camp's headquarters. The company had made a name for itself with canned pork and beans in tomato sauce.

I did introductions, and Cade made his pitch to product managers. They said no.

On the way out, we stopped unannounced into the office of Executive Vice President Hank Warren. He was a pretty tough guy who left no prisoners. We literally walked into his office, and I'm sure he steeled himself to get us out quickly. But he listened for twenty minutes. Then he called in his product managers—and overruled them. Stokely-Van Camp would acquire the rights to produce, market, and distribute Gatorade nationally. That was 1967, and it opened a whole new category of beverages: sports drinks.

Eventually, Gatorade's sales eclipsed all of the company's other products combined. Those product managers must have been chagrined. In the '80s, the brand was sold to Quaker Oats, which now is owned by PepsiCo.

Incidentally, Cade and his three colleagues who developed Gatorade formed a trust when Stokely-Van Camp bought the rights. By 2015, fifty years after the invention, royalties were estimated to have surpassed $1.1 billion. The University of Florida reaps 20 percent of the royalties.

No one actually *likes* to make a mistake. But mistakes will happen if you take risks. Or, in the case of the Stokely-Van Camp product managers, if you don't.

So here's a reminder to jot on a piece of paper and tape to your desk or tuck in a drawer:

> **When you make a mistake, there are only**
> **three things you should ever do about it:**
> **admit it, learn from it, and don't repeat it.**
>
> ———
>
> *Paul "Bear" Bryant*

CHAPTER 8

When to Pivot in Your Career

The young man was a brilliant copywriter. He was one of the best at J. Walter Thompson, a Manhattan-based advertising agency and pillar of the industry internationally. His future was secure and golden as he rose to lead the creative team.

But . . . he was bored. You can only get so much satisfaction from promoting green beans and decks of cards. He asked himself, "Am I really going to do this for the rest of my life?" And the answer was, "No—I want to do something else."

He came to me one day and asked, "What should I do?"

"What do you like doing?" I replied.

"Writing."

Eventually, he quit his promising advertising job and started writing novels.

To this day, James Patterson hasn't stopped writing books. His career change was good for him—he's sold more than 400 million copies—and for his legions of loyal readers.

How do you know when to pivot in your career? It can be a risky, though exhilarating, move.

I've always written decisions on a piece of paper. Longhand, with a nice pen. Pencils work, too, but it's too easy to erase a note and lose track of your thinking. Write down the pluses and minuses of your decision. If the pluses outweigh the minuses, then do it—and full speed ahead!

That sounds easy, but when you're deliberating a life-altering change, the process can be agonizing.

Sometimes the need for change is thrust upon you.

I joined Hill+Knowlton with all the enthusiasm of one holding a fresh graduate degree and ready to take on the world. The global public relations consulting company offered opportunity, and before long, I rose to working in the Manhattan headquarters. The clients we had were a who's who in American business. I loved my work and eventually became the president and CEO of the company. In my tenure, fee income nearly tripled. We had sixty-six offices in 125 countries. I had no desire to change.

But—and I bet you knew a "but" was coming—something happened.

I was "asked" by upper management in the parent company to do something I considered unethical. I quit, without another job lined up. This was September 1991, and newspapers wrote about my departure. I refused to say why I'd suddenly left, and this is the first time I've talked publicly about the reason. Personal integrity is important to me.

What was I going to do? How was I going to tell my wife, Jan, that I had walked away from a powerful and lucrative position? We had two young sons to raise.

I went to lunch one day at the Four Seasons and talked with August Busch, CEO of Anheuser-Busch, and Mike Roarty, his top marketing executive. They convinced me to take control of my fate and start my own public relations agency.

I walked out on 52nd Street and was going to walk all the way home to 87th and 5th. Despite what Busch and Roarty had encouraged me to do, I was terrified: I currently had no job and no income.

But by the time I got home, I had calls from Chase, W.R. Grace, Dun & Bradstreet, and Ford Motor Company—they all wanted to do business. Roarty had called them right after lunch; it was a tremendous help in those days.

Today, The Dilenschneider Group is going strong, with top companies and individuals as clients for more than three decades. I will always appreciate the advice that Busch and Roarty gave me and those calls that Roarty took the initiative to make.

Staying in your comfort zone is easy, but it's really important to get out of that zone and push the envelope. A move can be controversial; not everyone will like it. But if you do it, you'll feel better about your own persona, much better, and you actually might do some good along the way.

Elisa Verna, a software developer for thoughtbot, a Ruby on Rails consulting firm, put it this way in an interview for InHerSight: "I think we need to accept that you no longer need to work one career your whole life. Changing careers twice before thirty gave me so much confidence. I truly believe I can do anything if I work hard enough. I thought about becoming a nurse during the pandemic. Life is short, and we spend most of it working. Why have one career?"[1]

Ask yourself: Am I bored? Am I making a difference? Is there something I could be doing that could make a difference? Do I have a chance in my current job to motivate people, take them to a higher level? These are basic questions everyone should consider to determine if you need to try something different.

Ina Garten made that leap. Fans of her many cookbooks might be surprised to learn that in her twenties she was a staff member of the White House's Office of

Management and Budget. "There's got to be something more fun than this,"[2] she recalled in a 2016 *TIME* story.

"And then I saw an ad for a specialty-food store for sale in the *New York Times*, and it was in a place I'd never been before: West Hampton. So my husband, Jeffrey, said, 'Let's go look at it.' To say that I knew nothing about what I was getting myself into was an understatement. I'd never run a business before, never even had employees working for me. But when I saw the store, I thought, 'This is what I want to do.'"[3]

Being willing to take a risk, and listening to that inner voice, led to an astonishing career for one of America's most prolific cookbook authors, the host of the Food Network's *Barefoot Contessa*, the name of her shop.

Kim Malek realized she wanted something different from her career—she had been traveling from Seattle to New York almost weekly for her corporate job and instead "wanted to do something that was community based and where [she] could get to know [her] customers and employees and [her] neighbors and be home walking [her] dogs,"[4] she said in a 2018 interview with Shondaland, the television production company. It was a big risk when she eventually opened her first shop, especially since she'd drained her 401(k) for starter funds.

But she didn't let the risk of failing stop her. With a cousin, she cofounded Salt & Straw, an ice cream shop with specialty flavors that quickly became a hit. That was 2011. By 2022, there were thirty locations and annual revenues reaching the millions.

"I think when you're an entrepreneur, you have to believe in yourself blindly," Malek said, "and be willing to go and leap off a cliff and not know where you're gonna land."[5]

Do you believe in yourself? Are you willing to take a risk?

Don't be afraid to take a jump out of fear of going backwards, says Sheryl Sandberg, who early in her career went from a team of tens of thousands at the US Department of the Treasury to a team of just four at Google.

"There are so many times I've seen people not make that jump because they're afraid they'll . . . 'move backward,'" she said in the *When to Jump* podcast in 2017. "If you can financially afford it, and you're gonna work the next, I don't know, thirty years, who cares about 'going down?'"[6]

George Steinbrenner had it made. He didn't have to worry about "going down" in income. An industrialist, he ran a shipping company purchased by his great-grandfather out of Cleveland. He made a lot of money.

(He also misused some of that money and was convicted of making illegal campaign contributions to then-president Richard Nixon; later, President Ronald Reagan pardoned him.) But Steinbrenner decided he'd had enough of the shipping business, pivoted, and ended up acquiring and running the New York Yankees.

It wasn't just a matter of spending money but also a way of conducting himself that brought excitement to Yankee Stadium and players. Back then, when the national anthem was played, the teammates would mill around in the dugout. I asked him, why not have players stand at the first-base line, holding hats? Steinbrenner was a real patriot; he made it happen. He understood the significance of a gesture.

Rosalind "Roz" Brewer, the former COO of Starbucks, had a satisfying career with increasingly higher responsibilities. But then the COVID-19 pandemic happened.

"The pandemic was really hitting me at a certain point in my life at a time where I saw the virus impacting communities that needed some form of, first, education, and then to actually really get behind being vaccinated," she told *USA Today*. "So that first of all touched me, but what's most important is looking at it through a much longer-view lens and thinking about the health inequities across the United States."[7]

She left her stable, well-placed job and in 2021 became CEO of Walgreens Boots Alliance, just as the drugstore chain got involved, as other chains did, with helping to administer COVID-19 vaccines to save lives.

With her move, she became the highest ranking Black CEO on the Fortune 500 list of top executives in the country in 2022, ranks that surely need to grow, as the list includes only six Black CEOs.[8] She is using her prominence to draw attention to women who have had to leave the workforce during the pandemic because of responsibilities such as childcare.

———

If you decide it's time to change careers, then you'll need to come up with a plan. Start by focusing on what you enjoy doing the most. Why do you like it? What elements give you satisfaction? Then consider if you will need more education or certification. But before you enroll in an expensive program, do your research to determine whether that degree is actually necessary. If it is, can you pursue it after joining a company that contributes to its employees' education? Is there other training that will position you to get into a new field? Find a mentor who can advise you on what you need.

You may, however, already possess the skills for a different career.

At a glance, Koma Gandy was on a trailblazing career path. A midshipman in Naval ROTC at Harvard University, her first job was as a US Navy officer. She was among the first group of women assigned to combat ships. After four years of active duty, she went into the Navy Reserve but was recalled to active duty and deployed to the Gulf at the beginning of the Iraq War in 2003.

She then pursued her MBA and pivoted into financial services as an asset manager in New York City, teaching herself on the go about investment management, hedge funds, and financial operations. After a stint at Morgan Stanley, in 2019 she shifted again, this time into technology, and joined Codecademy, an online interactive site that offers free coding classes, as its vice president and head of curriculum.

"I have always applied the lessons of leadership and management I learned very early in my career to be successful in different industries, and consistently sought out opportunities to solve problems that make an impact," she said in an interview with InHerSight. "There's no 'one' perfect path—as long as you're learning all the time, finding new opportunities to grow, and working in places where you can meaningfully contribute to an organization (and be recognized for your impact), that's a good thing."[9]

Apply the lessons learned in chapter two on networking, and you will have a safety net when you decide if and when it's time to make a career leap. And above all else, remember my direction outlined in chapter one: know yourself.

As Michelle Obama has perceptively noted: "Sometimes the heart knows before the head."

CHAPTER 9

Protect Yourself and
Your Reputation

f you are reading this book and taking calculated chances as I suggest, there will be people who will want to take you down. They might try to sully your reputation—before you even realize this is happening. They might try to take advantage of you, such as with what I call an "image quack" or by posing as a friend. Outright lies about you could circulate—and get published.

Not to frighten you, but protecting yourself should be number one on your list.

The more power and influence you have, the greater the efforts of others to take them away—or at least take them down a few notches.

Here are a few things you should do right away *before* anything negative happens.

Look at your history with a gimlet eye. Make sure there's a reason for everything. For example, did you receive a speeding ticket when you were sixteen? Think of whether you had a reasonable explanation for it. (Late for work your first day at a paid job? That won't cut it. You should have planned ahead for traffic. You were a reckless teenager who didn't understand the power of the pedal? Well, at least that's honest. And you haven't had another ticket since, right?) Does it sound ridiculous that someone might dredge up an old speeding ticket? Well, let's say you've taken a public stand against drunk driving and support tougher laws. Someone could find out about your ticket—not knowing it was for speeding—and call you a hypocrite. It's easier to fix a problem before it becomes one.

Assume your life is an open book in this age of technology. Every reader should google themself—know what will come up and have explanations. Or, if something is outright false, get it removed from the online site.

Software tools can track platforms for any conversation about you. Then you can address any potential issues right away before your reputation is damaged. And it's not just you. This also pertains to your company. A complaint about your product on Twitter can go viral in hours and harm sales.

Look at what happened to General Mills in 2021. In March of that year, podcast host and comedian Jensen Karp tweeted a photo of what he said he found in a box of Cinnamon Toast Crunch cereal: two shrimp tails. "Ummmm @CTCSquares - why are there shrimp tails in my cereal? (This is not a bit),"[1] the tweet read.

That Twitter post got some attention—more than four thousand replies—but what made the tweet go viral was the company's response.

After offering to send Karp a replacement box of cereal, the social-media team tweeted that those weren't shrimp tails; they were cinnamon-sugar clumps: "After further investigation with our team that closely examined the image, it appears to be an accumulation of the cinnamon sugar that sometimes can occur when ingredients aren't thoroughly blended. We assure you that there's no possibility of cross contamination with shrimp."[2]

Keep in mind that Karp's tweet had included a photo, so thousands could see for themselves that the "accumulation" looked exactly like shrimp tails.

As can—and does—happen in the Twitterverse, a flood of ridicule and memes followed.

Soon, the shrimp tails leapt from Twitter to news stories in publications such as the *New York Times*, *Washington Post*, and *Business Insider* and broadcasts such as Fox News and CNN.

The Cinnamon Toast Crunch brand, owned by General Mills, had a crisis of embarrassing proportions on its hands. Some of this could not have been avoided, perhaps, but the company's response made it far, far worse.

The social-media team for Cinnamon Toast Crunch should have responded with the alacrity and seriousness appropriate for a matter of consumer health, even if it couldn't verify the contamination or quickly trace how it might have happened. In fact, one manager responded that it couldn't have happened in his facility, which sounded like passing the blame, not reassuring customers.

Instead of the ridiculous explanation of accumulated cinnamon sugar, the company could have responded by recalling all the boxes sold at Costco, where Karp had purchased his cereal. Stories like this live on via the internet, and if you Google "Cinnamon Toast Crunch," you'll see lots more sordid details.

If you see something negative, take it seriously. Even if, as could happen in other cases, it's patently not true.

I learned this lesson the hard way.

Many years ago, I was about to have the greatest honor any devout Catholic could receive: a meeting with the pope. It was to be at his summer residence, Castel Gandolfo, in Italy. But just before my dream was fulfilled, *Il Mondo*, Italy's leading business weekly, ran a story based on an anonymous source that "exposed" my supposed connection with Mikhail Gorbachev, the leader of the Soviet Union at the time. I denied any connection but didn't take the story seriously and didn't pursue a retraction because I knew it was completely untrue. However, the pope's staff deemed our meeting poor optics because of that story, and our meeting was cancelled. Later, the perception of this connection came back to haunt me with operatives who had assumed it was accurate. Believe me, it would have been easier to put out the fire initially.

———

I don't care who you are; everybody has somebody who doesn't like them. Usually, it has more to do with your position—your power—than with your personality. Figure out your list of detractors and know their agenda. Are they trying to erode your credibility? Lessen your influence? Block your project? Or even get your job? Criticism might come from out of nowhere.

If it's about your stand on an issue or a decision made for your company, then engage on that level. Do not argue. Explain and defend yourself in a positive way. If you disagree with someone, you can say you disagree. But it is important to disagree without making everyone upset.

Many years ago, I wanted to join a think tank, knowing I could make a contribution. The head of this nonprofit group did not like me, however, and he blocked every effort I made. I eventually gave up. My loss. Could I have avoided being turned down? Maybe. But I would still have had this guy against me. So I just moved on.

How can you tell that someone does not like you? Some signs are obvious. Are they trying to undercut your ideas or challenge every comment in a meeting? Maybe they don't smile when you're near or turn their back and ignore you when you walk by. They are not conversational and might respond to you with monosyllables—"no," "yes," "well"—without making eye contact.

How you handle such people depends on how often you must interact, whether you are their manager, and how much you need each other's support in the workplace. Always take the high road. Do not gossip about the other person or try to undermine them publicly (or privately, for that matter). Eyes open, mouth closed.

Betrayal can sting, but you must try to rise above it.

Melissa Dawn, the founder of CEO of Your Life and a certified life and business coach, believes that the negative of betrayal can be turned into a positive. Here's how she explains and visualizes one strategy:

"The way I see it, we're all on different floors of a building. Those who continuously work toward being their best selves are on a higher floor and possess higher-floor vibration. Those who focus on what isn't working and wallow in unhappy situations exist on lower floors with a lower-floor vibration," Dawn says. "If you maintain an upper-floor vibration, people look to you, wonder what you are doing, get curious, and start to raise their own vibrations. If, on the other hand, you lower your vibration to match theirs, you're not doing yourself (or anyone around you) any favors. Choose to go with your highest vibration, always. You'll feel better and proud of yourself, especially in the long run."[3]

Sometimes, as I did, you have to let go.

Let's face it—not everyone is going to like you. That may sound harsh, but likability is not your goal. You cannot please everyone and be an influential leader.

Less obvious is when someone is trying to manipulate you. An understanding of body language helps. Know the signs. Don Weber, a communications consultant, offers five tip-offs, excerpted here, in an October 2022 *Entrepreneur* article:[4]

- **Foot tapping:** "When somebody is tapping their feet, it is often a sign of annoyance or impatience. A manipulator may tap their feet, or start clicking a pen, to deliberately convey those emotions and cause their victim to feel guilt. Tapping the feet may also cause you to rush your decision which could play into a manipulator's best interest."

- **Chin scratching:** "When a manipulator scratches their chin, they are trying to show uncertainty or low confidence. This is often a tactic used to force people to give in and say, 'It's okay. I can just do it.'"

- **Hand and neck rubbing:** "Many people who feel stress will also rub their necks. It is possible for a manipulator to give signs of stress or guilt when exploiting another individual."

- **Eye contact and movement:** "It's commonly believed that if someone is looking you straight in the eye, they are telling you the truth. However, manipulators can hold eye contact for a long time. . . . Another important secret about a manipulator's eyes is the blink rate. Blinking can reveal what is going on in a person's neurology. An increased blink rate may indicate rising adrenaline, stress, or fear. Reduced blinking conveys more focus or relaxation, depending on the context of the situation."

- **Shifting body positions:** "If you sense that someone is trying to control you, begin to pay attention to how often they shift their body position. Shifting positions can be a manipulator's way of making you believe they are experiencing discomfort. Our minds are innately trained to recognize when a person is uncomfortable and provide consolation. As a result, you may be caving if someone is constantly moving their position."

These signs are not absolutes but are nevertheless something to watch for. Most importantly, notice unusual behavior—for example, when someone who is usually calm becomes fidgety.

How do you counter manipulations? Just by being aware. Don't capitulate if someone is subtly trying to make you do so.

Similarly, protect yourself from the "image quacks." These are the people who will try to sell you advice on a particular way to dress, to walk, to style your hair—like putting on a thin veneer. Remember the days, not that long ago, when the power handshake was the rage? Shake with a firm grip, then give an extra, quick squeeze. It's laughable now. But believe me, I've been at the receiving end of these handshakes more times than I can count. They come across as insincere. Be strong, be confident, and, most of all, be yourself.

When you have power and influence, others may try to be your friend. As I said in the networking chapter, professional relationships can be a key to ultimate success. But here's the caveat—know when someone is just a wannabe who wants to use you.

How can you identify such people? Ask them to do something small and see if they support you. Oftentimes, you need to know as much about the people you are dealing with as they know about you. That is the key to finding ways to protect yourself.

———

List your vulnerabilities, figure out what they are, and then take steps to reduce them.

But sometimes, it just may not be possible because of bad decisions you made along the way.

Bill Gates, a founder of Microsoft and one of the richest people in the world, presumably had it all. He was on top. He and his wife, Melinda French Gates, had formed a foundation to use their philanthropy for immense good in fields such as health care and education. But in 2021, Melinda filed for divorce, shocking many—and then the sordid details came out.

Bill confessed publicly that he'd had an affair with a Microsoft staffer years earlier. He apologized for hurting his wife and family. Of course, he had to come clean and try to take control of the narrative. But his reputation was sullied.

Is there more he should have done? You bet. He could have made a statement for all others who find themselves in situations like this, for one.

Once you realize things have changed, take stock of yourself. Deal with the various elements that shape your life. The issue of respect is important. Always speak well of other people. Anything negative you put out will come back to bite you.

It is important to have a good lawyer you can trust, a good doctor who will pay attention to you, and an investment advisor. Someone serious to move you in the right direction and not just put your money at risk. Ask your lawyer, your doctor, your investment advisor a pointed question. See how they respond and how much time it takes for them to get back to you. You need good people around you.

But sometimes you have no choice but to deal with the wrong people.

I was about to graduate from Ohio State University with my master's degree, and I'd earned a 4.0 GPA. The dean refused to give it to me.

"I never give higher than 3.95," was his explanation.

"But my grades were a 4.0," I reasoned.

"Three-point-nine-five is what you're going to get," he said, getting red in the face. "If you take it to a higher level, I'll reduce it more."

Why did he do that to me? I don't know. Maybe he felt my work wasn't quite up to it; maybe he didn't like me. I never found out why.

That one experience made me think twice. I had to take the 3.95.

The unforgettable lesson I learned is this: If you can't control the circumstance, you have to figure out a way around it—and still achieve what you want to achieve.

You are the master of your reputation. Care for it with diligence and insight, as only you can. Maintain your influence.

CHAPTER 10

How You Will Become a Memorable Manager

B arney Clark had an unforgettable style. Head of Delaware-based Columbia Gas when I knew him as a consultant, he had this end-of-the-day ritual: He would reach into a desk drawer, pull out a bottle of Jack Daniel's, place it on the desk, and pour out glasses. Then you would talk about all sorts of things. Clark was always plumbing for information.

"I'm confused," he would say if he didn't agree with my position. He would never say outright that he disagreed. His way of responding always helped me sharpen my thinking.

Now the days of keeping whiskey in a desk drawer are over, even for a CEO. But the lessons he taught me remain.

Always seek information, no matter how high up you are. Never attack another's position if you disagree. Instead, prod and poke it, elicit suggestions, listen to the defense. Be respectful of others' opinions.

This respect carried over into the way Clark interacted with his employees. Even though he ran a massive company, he knew employees' names and would ask about their families. He made a point of doing this five or six times a day. He knew what was important.

In this chapter, you will learn not only about being an effective manager, a winning manager, but also about how to be a *memorable* manager. There is a difference. You will see how to set the appropriate corporate culture, encourage ideas, and make them grow. How to be aware of biases and—this is crucial—how to make your company or organization more inclusive.

The COVID-19 pandemic has altered the corporate-office environment in lasting ways. You will need to make your management style effective in hybrid office–home workflow. This will involve heightened communication skills and implicit trust.

Even before the pandemic, societal factors were urging corporate leadership away from the timeworn top-down management style to something more collaborative. How did *you* like working for someone who always ordered everyone what to do? Sure, you completed your tasks, but likely your satisfaction was lacking. Top-down management gets the job done but stifles creativity—and ultimately can hold back the potential growth of a company or organization.

I believe the shift is for the better and implore you to be a part of it.

Perhaps there's a certain amount of relief in realizing that you, as a leader, do not have to hold all the answers. But in exchange, your leadership skill set must be even greater. You must *inspire*, not just motivate.

Larry Page, a cofounder of Google and billionaire many times over, knows this. "My job as a leader is to make sure everybody in the company has great opportunities, and that they feel they're having a meaningful impact and are contributing to the good of society,"[1] Page said.

How did Page do this? By paying employees more? Giving generous vacation time? Monthly pizza lunches?

He did it by making employees feel like family.

"It's important that the company be a family, that people feel that they're part of the company, and that the company is like a family to them," he said. "When you treat people that way, you get better productivity."[2]

Tami Longaberger knew instinctively that a great product is nothing without great people behind it. She took over the handmade maple-wood woven-basket company from her father, Dave.

The Longaberger Company's seven-story headquarters in Ohio was shaped like a huge basket. Quite a sight! The first time we met, we walked through the plant, and, every number of steps, we would stop and talk. She knew everybody there. It was hard to get through the plant, so many people wanted to talk with her. And she was gracious to each one.

The company that at its peak in 2000 had $1 billion in sales and 8,200 direct employees was acquired in 2013 and, five years later, closed. The following year, Xcel Brands relaunched the brand and expanded its offerings into other home goods and handcrafted items.

Longaberger continues her leadership as chair of the board of the Longaberger Family Foundation, which the website describes as "dedicated to the advancement of Appalachian Ohio, civics education, advancement of democratic values, and equal rights for all people."

Remember what I said about always trying to work for the betterment of society? Look for your own ways.

There are, of course, other ways to be a memorable leader.

Robert Crandall was tough as nails when he ran American Airlines in the 1980s and '90s and catapulted it into the leading airline in the United States at the time. He was called steel-edged, and his chain-smoking would now be derided, but he knew how to make his team comfortable in expressing its opinions. And he was a decent man who respected the views of others.

He would sit at the end of a long table and ask for ideas. Say someone would pose a suggestion, and someone else would dump on it. Crandall would say, "Wait a minute. Let's build on it." This is the essence of brainstorming.

You have to be open to ideas, to trends, to people. You might ultimately not accept a given idea, but leave it there. Respect it. Let people know that if you all can share ideas, you'll all be better for it.

Ray Dalio, the founder of the incredibly successful Bridgewater Associates hedge fund, puts it this way:

"If you want to be followed, either for egotistical reasons or because you believe it more expedient to operate that way, you will pay a heavy price in the long run," he writes in his book *Principles*. "Authoritarian managers don't develop their subordinates, which means those who report to them stay dependent. This hurts everyone in the long run. If you give too many orders, people will likely resent them, and when you aren't looking, defy them. The greatest influence you can have over intelligent people— and the greatest influence they will have on you—comes from constantly getting in sync about what is true and what is best so that you all the want the same things."[3]

You do this by nurturing a culture of creativity where people are encouraged to pitch ideas, be respectful of others, and feel valued. This doesn't come about overnight. But you certainly can—and should—cultivate it. Dalio's approach has produced the most successful company in his space and built a team of extraordinary individuals.

A memorable leader assumes the best of people. This is the highest form of respect, and your employees will be motivated to do their best because of it. May I add, this is a good direction for all parts of your life, not just the workplace. The world would be a much better, more civil place if everyone assumed the best of one another.

Tom Moran was a memorable manager because he was at once open and humble. Moran ran the insurance company Mutual of Omaha when I worked with him. You would never know he was the CEO—he was constantly giving the money he accumulated to others; he'd give you the shirt off his back. Moran never wanted applause.

He would call and say, "The IRA is in town, do you want to meet them?" And it wasn't that he had a political agenda; he was open to people and ideas. He was balanced and never took a side. Employees loved him.

People wanted to work for Sol Trujillo, a global media-communications and technology executive, at a number of companies, including Telstra. His style was not boisterous; he was very quiet and listened all the time. Only after listening would he make a decision. Most of all, he was downright nice.

He would say hello to everyone, including the shoeshine guy, and take the time for a chat. I once asked him why he did that.

"I was there once," he replied simply. "I was lucky enough to succeed. I have to give someone else the chance."

His kindness makes me think of something the national columnist David Brooks, who often writes about moral issues, famously said: "Success leads to the greatest failure, which is pride. Failure leads to the greatest success, which is humility and learning."

While great leaders ask others at many levels for their opinion and perspective before making major decisions, ultimately the call is up to them. The way a leader handles this can set them apart from the ordinary.

One of the most sensitive areas to navigate is when your decision differs from that of others. After all, a corporation is not a democracy where everyone gets an equal vote. But it is important that people can express their opinions and be respected.

For those in a position of responsibility and authority, like CEOs, a great many discussions are necessarily conducted with subordinates whose livelihood depends on one's continued goodwill, support, loyalty, and respect. It is precisely this imbalance in power that creates a peril for the CEO. As much as others depend on the CEO, the CEO must depend on them for the information and the considered opinions that it is their job to provide.

Yet if a CEO cannot conduct the discussion in a spirit of honest inquiry, the information and opinions that reach him will be distorted and generally worthless, and possibly counterproductive.

It is essential to foster a climate in which discussion and debate are conducted at the highest possible level, with no fear of expressing one's opinions and without harsh consequences for being wrong. Those leaders who ignore these imperatives tend to be surrounded by yes-men. It is no doubt pleasant to have one's own views constantly echoed and applauded by subordinates. But an effective leader needs to have no-men (and no-women)—those who are able and willing to disagree—close at hand.

A top executive needs to listen and learn. But what if you do not agree with someone? There is a way to tell them without turning them off. For example: "Jack, I hear and appreciate your view but, respectfully, will go another way on this issue."

Be up-front, sincere, respectful, and appreciative of the advice, even if you don't ultimately follow it.

———

One of the biggest challenges for a manager is within the company: how to attract and retain the best employees. And the answer may be within you.

"A majority of employees leave their employers due to management and failures to lead,"[4] notes Kedma Ough, CEO of Target Funding (and author of the book by the same name). As a consultant, some of the common reasons for leaving that she's heard from departing employees have been:

"I didn't feel heard or respected."

"There was no clarity in my part in the greater strategy."

"My manager didn't support my growth."[5]

She recommends incorporating critical, but often overlooked, training areas into your organization's structure, such as "effective communication and conflict management; skill building, aligned with individual responsibilities and career plan; alignment to corporate objectives and putting shared principles into practice; [and] leadership-skills development, based on establishing trust and rapport."[6]

Let me underscore this point. Ongoing training is vital to helping your employees feel valued and to maintaining the appropriate culture. Do this through challenges. See what people come up with as solutions. It will pay big dividends. You must invest in your employees, and they, and the wider organization, will benefit.

Indra Nooyi, the former CEO of PepsiCo, had ways—and the patience—to attract people and take them from that first step up to the tenth. She was and still is very determined and very smart. She would say no to people, but in a pleasant way.

Aside from her style and brilliance, she attracted top-notch people through the daring mission she developed for the company. She was intent on reshaping PepsiCo, the ubiquitous soda firm that also owned snack brands such as Lay's potato chips, into a health-conscious and environmentally sensitive organization. Think about it: She wanted to change a hugely successful company associated with snacks—filled with sugar, fat, and/or salt—into one perceived as healthy! Radical. And gutsy.

And precisely the kind of ambitious goal that made her extraordinary as a leader.

She called her idea Performance with Purpose, which would become the umbrella for everything the company would do. Her daunting task was to get everyone to buy into it.

"We would deliver excellent performance, as was expected for PepsiCo, but would add three imperatives to our work ahead: nourish humanity, and the communities in which we live; replenish our environment; and cherish the people in our company."[7]

She hired scientists who would formulate less sugary drinks and less salty snacks while maintaining flavor. Manufacturing was reconfigured to use less water in the process, and bottles contained recycled material.

"Good business demands tough decisions based on rigorous analysis and unwavering follow-through. Emotion can't really play a part," she said. "The challenge we all face as leaders is to let the feelings churn inside you but then to present a calm exterior, and I learned to do that."[8]

Nooyi stayed calm when, early in her leadership tenure, she would look around the table and see she was the only woman and the only immigrant.

She set about to make leadership more reflective of a diverse society. At one point, she asked HR to find more diverse candidates. They came back with a handful of Canadians. This was not going to be easy.

Diversity and inclusion have become buzzwords in recent years, but they are critically important to a thriving corporate culture. As a leader, you must be committed to creating an inclusive culture.

It should be obvious that viewpoints brought by people of various genders, ethnicities, religions, ages, sexual preferences, and more are valuable and create a vitality. But the obvious can elude us because of cognitive bias. Our particular experiences can blindside us. You must be aware of this and be constantly vigilant. Be open to views that are not yours. This is vital in business and valuable in life.

Phil Bohlender, an international consultant who is openly gay, offers three areas that every leader can act on to build an inclusive leadership style.

Trust: Working with people who have different skillsets who know how to do their jobs and create the expected outcomes. *Empowerment:* Inviting people to work on new things that build skills and stretch their scope. *Collaboration*: Partnering with people to work together who have complementary skills.[9]

Inclusive leaders should also incorporate these traits into their unique leadership style: integrity, influence, and impact. You'll notice these are three "I"s—but really, it's all about "we."

Inclusion and diversity will, and must, be among the cornerstones for corporations and organizations. They are not a human resources fad that will fade out in a year or two (such as, for example, requiring every employee to wear a printed mission statement on a fob around their neck).

"Diversity is not an issue that just affects minorities or women," notes Karen Horting, executive director and CEO of the Society of Women Engineers. "Diversity is an issue that affects the entire workforce."[10]

The way you make your organization more inclusive—and your sincere commitment to it—will make you a memorable leader.

———

You must be super vigilant about inclusion as corporations and organizations emerge from the COVID-19 pandemic with new work systems that likely will remain in some form.

Hybrid working—part of the week from home, a few days in the office—brings benefits but also challenges. You have to keep employees engaged and make sure they have equal access to development, no matter where they are working.

Trust, as I've said over and over again, is crucial.

Elaine Thomley, a vice president in financial planning and analysis at Synchrony, a consumer financial-services company formerly known as GE Capital with net income of $4.2 billion in 2021, believes hybrid working can be effective.

"I'm not afraid of being overlooked for a career opportunity, because the directive to move to this new way of working comes from the very top: our CEO and his direct reports," she wrote in a 2022 op-ed. "Our senior executives support the new model because it has created a more effective, collaborative, and loyal workforce. Employees are happy they can integrate work into their lives in a way that doesn't relegate life to the losing end of the bargain."[11]

The pandemic has underscored that managers must be constantly able to adapt to changing circumstances, even unforeseen ones. But some traits and values do not shift. Within the many different leadership styles, certain characteristics are common to all influential leaders.

Focus your energies. Set priorities. (The manager's priorities are clear symbols for others in an organization to follow.) Never make excuses; take responsibility. Be positive—but realistic. Inclusive with generating ideas—but decisive. Be bold—but willing to shift gears if the bold plan doesn't work. Always be respectful and appreciative. Be principled. Like what you are doing. And inspire. And, if needed, admit you were wrong.

You will be the memorable manager.

CHAPTER 11

The Inevitable Crisis:
Know How to Handle It
and Benefit

While you can follow tips to predict trends, you can't predict a crisis. Yet, one will come. Without a doubt, one will come.

What you *can* do, and *must* do, is be prepared.

Pay attention to this chapter, and you will not only navigate any crisis, but you will also see how to turn it into an opportunity.

"You never want a serious crisis to go to waste," noted Rahm Emanuel, former Chicago mayor and chief of staff to President Barack Obama during the 2008–09 recession. "And what I mean by that is an opportunity to do things that you think you could not do before."

To this day, the way Johnson & Johnson handled the Tylenol crisis remains the gold standard on what to do and is a case study still taught in universities four decades later. Seven people had died in the Chicago area in 1982 after taking Extra Strength Tylenol capsules that had been poisoned with cyanide. It had been J&J's best-selling product and dominated the painkiller market.

"What set apart Johnson & Johnson's handling of the crisis from others? It placed consumers first by recalling 31 million bottles of Tylenol capsules from store shelves and offering replacement product in the safer tablet form free of charge,"[1] explained the *New York Times* in a reflective piece on the twentieth anniversary of the poisonings. I was directly involved in developing a solution. The company responded with tamper-proof packaging—which changed the industry—and though the recall and relaunch cost $100 million, J&J's share of the lucrative analgesic market quickly rebounded close to what it had been before the crisis.

A lot of companies would have cut and run, which is a big mistake.

Lesson number one: If public health is at risk, respond immediately and decisively. Don't evade responsibility, even if the crisis is not of your company's making. Sabotage led to the tampered Tylenol, not the company's actions. The perpetrator remains a mystery.

Lesson number two: know exactly what you are responding to. Action in a crisis must be commensurate with the threat.

Here's an example of what I mean by that. The safety of fruit imported from Chile was being challenged by the US Food and Drug Administration in 1989. Acting on an anonymous tip, an FDA inspector in Philadelphia made a special examination of a miniscule portion of the hundreds of thousands of tons of fruit brought in daily.

Two grapes in 600,000 crates were found to be injected with cyanide.

The FDA commissioner was about to ban the sale of Chilean grapes when a lawyer called me to help the Chilean government deal with the impending crisis. We went to work quickly and made sure the Chilean government was able to present a single consistent position to the Department of Commerce, Federal Trade Commission, and FDA. We reinforced with the FDA the risk of inappropriately submitting to terrorist demands. The real villains were unknown, but the victims would be the American consuming public and the fruit growers of Chile.

Was the danger to the public real? Fortunately, no. If it had been, we would have handled the situation differently. No other contaminated grapes had ever been found. We were able to convince the FDA to lift its ban and then broadened the field of information to include the trade, the industry, consumers, and the media and demonstrated to them the absurdity of being bamboozled by two grapes in 600,000 crates. We were careful, however, to never try to dismiss the public's fear directly.

What you have to do, especially if you are dealing with an unsafe-product situation, is to take a deep breath and then see if the panic is warranted. If it isn't, then you can isolate the fear, step by methodical step, and counteract it.

That said, you must also be proactive and prepare for a crisis *before* it happens.

Jonathan Dedmon, a principal with The Dilenschneider Group who now heads my Miami office, describes steps to take in a chapter on crisis communications he wrote for *The Public Relations Handbook*, which I edited and was published in 2022.

"The first step is to establish a core team that can manage crises effectively right when they occur," Dedmon writes. The team should include the CEO and/or the COO, legal counsel, and public/media relations. Other senior executives can be added, but keep the number to ten or fewer. You need to be nimble.

Take an inventory of past crises in your company or industry and determine whether they might reoccur.

Come up with a written plan on how the company will respond—before any crisis happens. This should be short, only a few pages. It should include a brief statement that the company will address the problem with honesty and transparency, act in the public interest, and have empathy for those affected. Also, include the names and contact information of the core-team members and the responsibilities for communication with all key stakeholders, along with their contact information. These may be employees, customers, suppliers, government officials, and the media. The group should meet annually to review and update the plan.

You are now as prepared as you can be for the unknown.

When a crisis strikes, your core team must assess the seriousness of the situation. Define what the crisis is, what the effects are, and what needs to be done to solve it.

Monitor reactions in social media, with employees and customers, to the stock price and Wall Street commentary, any government involvement, and media inquiries, including their nature and tone.

In the early stages of a crisis, often the first day, the best strategy is to tell it all and tell it fast. Be disciplined and know that nothing happens automatically. The crisis could take hours, even months.

Make sure everyone on your team knows the message. Make it concise.

"It is a generally accepted rule," Dedmon writes, "that the best messaging has a strong emotional component versus simply a logical and rational argument."

- Talk from the viewpoint of your audience and to their self-interest.
- Avoid jargon and euphemisms. An explosion is not an incident.
- Tell the truth, even if it hurts. Don't be defensive.
- If the media gets something wrong, correct it immediately.
- Never say, "No comment." If the information is private—say, about personnel—explain the reason. Then find something else to say.

Decide who will speak for the company. Identify at least one person. But it might need to be a few people, such as someone to respond to media and someone else—preferably a top executive—to speak to employees. Preparation should include what difficult questions are likely to be asked so that you can be ready with answers.

If a press conference is one of the strategies, then make sure the setting establishes the right tone.

———

While Johnson & Johnson's handling of the Tylenol scare is a model for the right way to address a scandal, Volkswagen provides the opposite: the wrong way.

Volkswagen was accused by the Environmental Protection Agency in 2015 of deliberately violating the Clean Air Act through software that permitted its cars to pass emissions tests. Eco-friendly? Customers felt like that was a sham, and no one likes to be misled. Trust was shattered.

Company executives bungled the response. Initially, they said they didn't know about the cheating, only to later admit they did. Then the company moved to lay off 300,000 workers. While this might have been unrelated to the scandal, the perception was that employees who had nothing to do with it were being fired to make up for the loss in profits.

Consumers took to social media to charge the company with deliberately deceiving them.

It takes a long time, if ever, to repair this type of damage to a company's reputation and to rebuild trust.

A crisis might not be of your company's doing, but poorly handled or not addressed properly, the response could make everything worse.

It was not Amazon's fault that a tornado destroyed one of its warehouses in Edwardsville, Illinois, in December 2021, part of a series of violent tornadoes that tore through parts of four states. Six people died in the warehouse. But the company gave a delayed response to the tragedy. Twenty-four hours would pass before CEO Jeff Bezos tweeted a statement. It came across as insincere. (A side note: wording is crucial.)

Part of Bezos's tweet was "our thoughts and prayers are with their families and loved ones."[2] The phrase "thoughts and prayers" has become overused by politicians responding to mass shootings while refusing to pass meaningful gun violence–prevention legislation. Bezos should have chosen other words.

The crisis spiraled as reports came out that workers allegedly were forced to continue working through tornado warnings. The Occupational Health and Safety Administration investigated and ultimately determined in April 2022 that the company had met minimum guidelines for dealing with severe weather; no fine was issued.

A crisis might be something happening outside your industry but can open the opportunity to respond with principled action.

When the US Supreme Court struck down the nearly fifty-year-old *Roe v. Wade* decision in June 2022, protests erupted nationwide, fueled by anger that women's rights were being taken away. A majority on the court determined that states could decide whether to allow or restrict abortion. A number of companies, such as Apple, Disney, and Dick's Sporting Goods, responded quickly with the offer to pay employees for travel-related expenses if they had to go out-of-state for an abortion procedure. Other companies, such as Amazon, Netflix, and Starbucks, announced similar policies the month before when a memo on the decision was leaked.

These major corporations were taking strong stands in support of employees. Within days of the decision, a CBS poll showed that a majority of Americans supported abortion. But with such a controversial topic, not everyone sees the Supreme Court decision as a disaster. Once the corporations took their bold position, there's no backing down.

A few words on dealing with the media.

Never dodge it.

If the crisis is a tragedy, then reporters will have to write or broadcast stories no matter what. You can't completely control the narrative, but you can make sure the company's message is heard. Know that in a half-hour interview, only two or three quotes are likely to be used, so keep your message succinct and repeat it.

The way to deal with the media in a crisis is to have developed a relationship beforehand. Who are the respected journalists covering your industry? Who are the reporters and editors of the local newspapers and television stations your employees are likely to read or watch? You should know this information. Feed a reporter something interesting (not self-serving) going on in your company or industry. Tip them off when a big announcement is about to be made, such as a change in leadership or relocation of headquarters. Answer calls and emails. Building trust in the good times will prove a valuable foundation in a time of crisis.

Take it a step further and cultivate third parties who can help create credibility. These could include experts on an issue, academics, scientists, think tanks, and opinion leaders.

When the crisis has passed, gather your core team and assess what you've learned and what could have been done better. Then adjust your plan for dealing with the next one.

CHAPTER 12

Predicting Trends:
Your Key to
Keeping Power

There's no way you could lock in trends every year for twenty years. Without a doubt, things will go in a different direction—and likely involve something that doesn't even exist today.

But good leaders do not sit back and respond only to what's in front of them. If you do that, you and your company will be left in the dust. Look at Kodak. Once the undisputed leader in film, the company didn't anticipate in time the quick shift to digital. And now, of course, high-quality cameras are built into our cell phones. Who would have foreseen that a few decades ago?

If you have followed the lessons in previous chapters of this book, you'll be well on your way to leading with power and influence. Now you will learn key tips for maintaining and growing those aspects.

"You can accurately predict enough of the future to make all the difference. In fact, you can hone your ability to trigger a burst of accurate insight about the future and use it to produce a new and radically different way of doing things," writes author and futurist Daniel Burrus. "Called a flash foresight, this is about looking into the future and transforming it into a new paradigm for solving 'impossible' problems, unearthing 'invisible' opportunities, and running extraordinarily successful businesses in the twenty-first century."[1]

Sounds good, right? Here are some tools to get you there.

Look at hard trends, not just cyclical changes. An example of a hard trend might be that people are having fewer children. (The US birth rate fell by 4 percent from 2019 to 2020, the Centers for Disease Control and Prevention reported, the sharpest single-year decline in almost fifty years and the lowest number of births since 1979.)[2]

Consider what the hard trends mean for what *will*—not just *might*—be needed. How can you and your company adapt? What kind of organization can you form to meet the upcoming consequences and beat your competitors?

Lee Iacocca, the head of Chrysler, saw that baby boomers were an untapped market for a new type of vehicle they didn't know yet wanted. The company had been struggling financially, and the US government had guaranteed a $1.5 billion loan. Iacocca designated nearly half of that amount for the project, and in November of 1983, the Dodge Caravan was introduced—the first minivan and an entirely new category of personal transport.

Early ads described the Caravan as "one vehicle that takes the place of an economy car, sporty car, station wagon, and van."[3] The Caravan was an immediate success, and Chrysler was on top of the market for a solid fifteen years.

But tastes and sensibilities—and consumers' penchant for something different—led Chrysler (now known as Fiat Chrysler) to discontinue the Grand Caravan line in 2020. SUVs replaced them in the market, and now hybrid and electric vehicles are poised to revolutionize transportation.

Look at the global stage. It is helpful for you and your business to decipher where the power will be centered. Once, it was predicted that China would be the super economic power, taking on the United States in that role, with Russia close on the heels. However, Vladimir Putin's ill-advised and ill-executed invasion into Ukraine in early 2022 made Russia an outcast among NATO countries.

China still sees itself dominating this century, much as the United States did in the previous century. I would never discount our country, but I am predicting here—based on my research—that the power to watch for is India.

One strategy I like for anticipating trends is to analyze what others are doing—and do the opposite. Isn't that counterintuitive? You bet.

"One way to help tease . . . insight to the surface is to note what everyone else is thinking and doing—and then look in the opposite direction," advises Burrus. "Jeff Bezos looked at how Barnes & Noble had taken the traditional bookstore to a new level of size and substance, creating the modern superstore, and went the other way: he shrank the size to nothing and made it completely insubstantial."[4]

Anticipate and prepare.

"In the twenty-first century, the one and only thing you can depend on is transformation," Burrus continues. "This means you can't go backward, and you can't stand still; you can't rest on your laurels, and you can't keep doing what you've always done, even if you do your best to keep doing it better. The only way to survive, let alone thrive, is to continuously reinvent and redefine. Reinvent and redefine what? Everything."[5]

Indra Nooyi could have rested on her laurels for a while. After all, General Electric and PepsiCo simultaneously were pressing her with attractive job offers in the 1990s. Even though PepsiCo's restaurant leg of the business included KFC, Taco Bell, and Pizza Hut—she wondered whether she could relate, however, because she didn't eat meat—she ultimately chose PepsiCo. She became senior vice president of corporate strategy and planning for the corporation, which was composed of beverage, snack, and restaurant businesses.

She could have downplayed her recommendation, after careful analysis, to divest the restaurant portion of the business; she could have been satisfied with gains against major competitor Coca-Cola. But she didn't downplay, and she wasn't satisfied with "good enough." She noticed a trend.

"Health and wellness, to me, was undeniably a category that offered huge opportunity,"[6] she writes in her memoir *My Life in Full*. How was she convinced? Early on, by noticing what was happening at her young daughter Tara's birthday party.

"I found it more than curious that a couple of children at Tara's birthday party one year asked if they could phone their mothers to get permission to sip Pepsi we served. That sent up a real red flag for me."[7]

She guided PepsiCo into healthy drinks and food, such as products with less sugar, fats, and salt, and environmental responsibility, which included using less water for producing beverages. "I believe that a company's impact on society needs to be written through all business planning and that this cannot be an after-thought. Performance with Purpose. With PwP, I had a strategy—simple and thoughtful—to take PepsiCo into the future."[8]

Frank Luntz knows the importance of research. If you don't do your research, your business could go down the wrong path, and it could get too late to turn it around. A consultant, Luntz has written, supervised, and con-ducted more than 2,500 surveys, focus groups, ad tests, and dial sessions in more than two dozen countries; he's absolutely brilliant and the best researcher in the world I've ever met.

Not only is research essential for spotting and prepar-ing for trends, but it's also useful for helping you pitch the right message about, for example, a new direction for your company.

Take the notion of security, for example. "Most busi-nesses talk about how their products and services give you a sense of 'security.' But that just means that there's a threat out there from which they are protecting you. If you talk about 'peace of mind,' that means there are no threats, that you can close your eyes, relax, and not worry," Luntz writes in the 2022 edition of *The Public Relations Handbook.* (Full disclosure: I created the idea for the book and then edited it.)

Through his research, Luntz found out where people were, told them how to move from that step to another, and then did research at the end to see if they achieved it. People in a company didn't always like this consultant coming in and telling them to change their way of thinking. But if everything is always coming from your point of view, what about your customers' point of view? That's your chance for moving the ball into the future.

In my own life, I've tried as hard as I can to listen to other people. You've got to listen; that's the key. A lot of people don't like to listen—they'd rather talk.

Although predicting trends could rely on trying to anticipate what isn't invented yet, you can also think counterintuitively and look back.

"If you want to know what the trends of tomorrow will look like, then you should study up on the trends of yesterday. Trends work as a chain reaction in a way," Melissa South, senior vice president for the retailer SwingTie, suggested in an Enterprise League article. "When popular things randomly disappear, you cannot expect them to stay gone forever. Nostalgia is a strong tool that everyone should keep their eyes on. If you notice something fading away, remember that people once loved it, and over time that love can come back again."[9]

Overall, be curious. Like Nooyi, notice what's going on right in front of you. It could indicate a bigger trend coming like a wave on the horizon.

CHAPTER 13

How You Can Lead the Changing Workplace

Alan Mulally stepped into an enormous challenge when he became head of the Ford Motor Company in 2006. The storied car manufacturer was on the verge of bankruptcy with multibillion-dollar losses. What kind of leader would it take to turn this company around?

Intelligence and creativity were givens. So were a sense of responsibility and a belief in the product, in its value and benefits to the consumer. What set Mulally apart and made him uniquely qualified for this monumental task?

He could inspire others. He didn't issue edicts, though he certainly could have. He could have been a task-oriented leader and perhaps gotten the job done. Instead, he involved others at the company in decisions—he was people-oriented. He underscored the importance of everyone, at every level and in every function, to work together to achieve common goals. They had to understand the vision and feel optimistic about the company in order to give their all.

He drew people in. He sought ideas from employees—not just his management circle—and customers. Though he clearly was in power, he was also humble. He considered it an honor to serve.

"*Positive* leadership—conveying the idea that there is always a way forward—is so important, because that is what you are here for—to figure out how to move the organization forward. Critical to doing that is reinforcing the idea that everyone is included. Everyone is part of the team and everyone's contribution is respected, so everyone should participate," Mulally said in a 2013 interview with McKinsey & Company. "When people feel accountable and included, it is more fun. It is just more rewarding to do things in a supportive environment."[1]

Within three years of Mulally becoming Ford's CEO, the company was posting profits annually. That's a remarkable turnaround.

The workplace and the world are changing in various ways for multiple reasons. In this chapter, you will learn how to adapt—and thrive. The smart executive has to be prepared to apply skills to evolving environments. In other words, you can't be stuck in your ways. Mulally knew that. What worked for you or your company last year might not work for you next year.

The first step is to be aware and accurately informed about what is going on in the world. Not only about the global economy and influences on it but also about politics, culture, science, religion, climate, and more. Pay attention to what is happening around you, in your own life and in the larger world. Ignorance of reality cannot possibly lead to good decisions. You cannot be intellectually isolated and lead effectively.

You are required to have an understanding of relevant issues and what forms them. The ability of somebody or some organization to stimulate a point of view or a new idea has reached an all-time high, and it's going to continue and get worse. Get your facts; form your own opinions. You have to be able to cut through the falsehoods, the half-truths, and get to the real truth. Develop a short ledger of facts that are irrefutable. And—I am absolutely adamant on this—don't rely on one source for information.

Gone are the days when the *New York Times* was the bible for news. It's reputable, but you do need to know what's reported in the *Wall Street Journal*, too, for example. I read or skim thirty newspapers from around the world every day. You can see trends developing that way.

Never watch only one news network and consider yourself knowledgeable. You would be limiting yourself, and that is terribly foolish.

While I'm encouraging you to think globally, you need to understand on a basic level that some countries resent the West and actively try to undermine it.

I remember meeting Aleksandr Solzhenitsyn; he came to New York from Georgia. We were sitting one night in a coffeehouse and talking openly about lots of things.

"You realize when I go back, I can never talk like this again," he said to me. "My days are numbered."

I don't think he knew what was going to happen. But it was a chilling reminder that we have freedoms in this country that are taken for granted.

As the world is changing—fueled by technology and instantaneous communication and shaped by aggressive countries seeking power—so is the workplace shifting in ways unforeseen even a few years ago.

The COVID-19 pandemic upended the very workplace itself as, in many professions, employees were forced to work from home—and liked it. As companies tried to move back to "normal" workday office hours, hybrid models became more than a temporary transition. More women are reaching upper management—although still not at sufficient levels—and advocate for changes to childcare, among other areas. "Work-life balance" is a buzz phrase, as is "quiet quitting." And a new generation is entering the workforce with different ideas and motivations.

You must do more than just navigate these changes. You must—and can—lead in the new realities. And be prepared for even more, as yet unknown, changes to come.

This might sound paradoxical, but this type of leadership is rooted in your bedrock values. (For more on values, go back to chapter one.) Continue to give attention to your conscience, your core values, your principles. These are what will give you true guidance.

Write down your core values. You might ask: Why is this important—isn't it enough to just know them? When they're written down somewhere, you can check now and then to make sure your behavior is consistent with those values. When they are aligned, they become your compass, and your unique purpose (or purposes) becomes achievable.

———

No longer do people stay at one job and retire with a gold watch. Hardly. More than forty million Americans quit their jobs in 2021, most moving on to other positions. Since most companies no longer have defined pension plans, employees feel empowered to leave for other places and take their 401(k) with them. While mobility might be good for the employee (and that includes you as a CEO), such churn makes it difficult to run a company. Institutional memory is lost. Skill sets need constant training to get to previous levels. And that entire process is expensive, reaching into the millions of dollars every year.

Employee annual voluntary turnover in the United States was likely to jump nearly 20 percent in 2022, going from an annual average of 31.9 million to 37.4 million quitting their jobs in 2022, according to Gartner, Inc.[2]

A study by Work Institute in 2020 zeroed in on why employees quit. The top three categories for leaving were career development (20 percent), work–life balance (12 percent), and manager behavior (12 percent).[3]

As a leader, what can you do to satisfy these concerns and retain your valued employees? Do you have enough pathways for advancement in your company? How could you improve the sense of work–life balance? (Here's one clue: stop sending emails after midnight—unless there's a crisis. And then you should call.) Does your company culture encourage creativity or lead to burnout?

Are you building a culture of problem-solvers? Make it conducive for your people not to be afraid to speak up, to feel empowered. Their suggestions may not always be taken, as I've said before, as the ultimate decision rests with you—but they must feel that they can speak honestly and be heard.

———

Loyalty can seem old-fashioned to young people as they switch jobs to get ahead, but loyalty can—and should—still be cultivated. Even brand loyalty has to be fought for and often doesn't last, replaced by the latest trend, the newest fad.

Some of this is good, actually. Why be loyal to a brand that fails to live up to our expectations, to a cause that disappoints us, to a person who abuses our trust? No one wants to be taken for a fool.

But not being able to trust and not expecting loyalty in any aspect of our lives is a frightening, unsustainable state of affairs. Being realistic is one thing, but not feeling loyalty to anyone or anything is dehumanizing.

How to translate this into the workplace? As with so many facets of managing, your efforts must be genuine.

Factors that contribute to a workplace where employees will want to stay and do their best vary, but overall, "an empathic boss, upper management's caring attitude, a relaxed and productive atmosphere, financial benefits, job security, commitment to excellence, and open and honest communication" plus opportunities for growth are important, writes Bryan Robinson in a 2022 article for *Forbes* describing "what makes an appealing workplace."[4]

Your employees at every level need to see how they can advance and feel supported and guided on that path by supervisors on up. If more training opportunities are required, that very well could be a worthwhile investment. You will be retaining employees and cultivating loyalty.

Belief in senior leadership—its competence, fairness, engagement with workers, and eagerness to see them succeed—is one of the strongest factors in employee loyalty.

———

Another change in the workplace is an infusion of younger people. Millennials, those born between 1981 and 1996, are the fastest-growing segment of the workforce.

As you very well might find yourself managing at least three and perhaps up to five distinct generations, you need to know what motivates each. Some are common, such as respect, and others are generational.

Jennifer Herrity, a career coach, denotes it this way in a 2022 Indeed article: Traditionalists, people born between 1928 and 1945, may comprise a small portion of the current workforce, but some born in the later years are still there. They value loyalty and make an effort to help others. They have a strong work ethic but likely prefer not to work at nontraditional times such as weekends or nights. "This generation often enjoys human connections and may be more productive if they have the opportunity to engage in person with peers,"[5] says Herrity.

Baby boomers, born between 1946 and 1964, once the largest part of the population, are often comfortable taking risks. They make good mentors. "Many members of this generation are approaching retirement age, so they often value flexible work schedules. Many experienced employees may consider working longer if managers could provide them with reduced schedules, the chance to work from home, or flexible hours,"[6] Herrity explains.

Generation X, born between 1965 and 1980, have common traits of independence and personal development. They often prefer more autonomy in their work. "These professionals value a healthy work–life balance and prefer working for companies that offer monetary awards, such as bonuses and company stock options,"[7] Herrity notes.

Millennials, born between 1981 and 1996, were the first to grow up with technological advancements and so are savvy about using them. They often value quality performance and are not hesitant to challenge authority. "Skills mentorship and consistent feedback are helpful for this generation to achieve longevity at a company, and this might help managers make strategies to improve the skills of their team,"[8] Herrity says.

And finally we have Generation Z, born between 1997 and 2015, beginning to enter the workforce. They value authenticity, truth, and relationships and expect that from their managers. "They often like flexible working hours and workplaces that value diversity and social responsibility,"[9] Herrity adds.

As you can see, each generation approaches the job differently, but when you know how you can help them all work optimally—which everyone wants—then you can strengthen the entire workplace.

It's the millennials and younger people who are driving change, which benefits workers of all generations, notes Alan Murray, the CEO of Fortune Media, in his book *Tomorrow's Capitalist: My Search for the Soul of Business*, published in 2022.

"In this environment, we can envision workforce empowerment as three points of a triangle," he writes. "The first is training workers to take advantage of opportunities supplied by new technologies. The second is delivering a living wage to all workers. And third is creating a workplace with human values."[10]

As Whole Foods cofounder John Mackey writes in his book *Conscious Capitalism*, "Most people in the twenty-first century . . . want to work for more than just a paycheck."[11]

Reshma Saujani, founder and CEO of Girls Who Code, would agree.

"I ended up working at a law firm and then in finance, at jobs that I hated that paid enough to pay off my loans and to help my parents with their mortgage. I was seriously depressed and miserable because I was not giving back to the world. The money wasn't making me happy, and I felt more and more beholden to it, more and more scared," she told the *Atlantic* in July 2018. "No longer will I work in a job that I hate for a paycheck."[12]

Do you know the single best strategy for retaining young employees? Include them in the decision-making. Make them feel their worth. Help them develop a stake in the company and feel that what they are doing is ethically responsible.

Let me give you an example . . . of how *not* to do it.

At Weyerhaeuser, the American timberland and wood-products company, a manager named Don Janicke terrified people. He would tell everybody in the room,

"This is the way it's going to be done—or else." George Weyerhaeuser, who started the company, would never have tolerated Janicke's management style.

Eventually, three or four young people came up to him and said they wanted to be heard. Or they would leave.

They wanted to give Janicke a chance, but they had to be included. As you have read, that's critically important in general for millennials. Wisely, he adjusted his autocratic style.

Nurture an environment in which people can safely speak honestly and want to help each other succeed.

As I've said before, a good manager doesn't have to have all the answers. That's impossible over the long term. But you have to listen with an open, yet challenging, mind. And then have the rectitude to make a decision—and take responsibility for it.

Let's not automatically assume that the newest generation in the workforce has a lot to learn before they can be fully effective. Many people in their early twenties have already made substantial contributions.

Consider Malala Yousafzai. She did not have the goal to be honored as an activist for girls' education in Pakistan. Her goal was to defend her right and that of other girls in her village to go to school. When the Taliban came to power, the fundamentalist group issued an edict against educating girls. But Yousafzai followed the courage of her convictions. For that, in 2012 when she was fifteen, she was shot in the head while riding a school bus.

Miraculously, she survived, recuperated in England, and continued her education, which was so important to her. She wanted other girls to have the opportunity to learn, too, and continued to speak out. She was awarded the Nobel Peace Prize in 2014 for her "struggle against the suppression of children and young people and for the right of all children to education."

You can read about her remarkable story in her own words in her book *I Am Malala*.

Young people everywhere are standing up for what they believe in. Greta Thunberg, the Swedish environmental activist, is just one example. She was not yet twenty when she began standing outside the Swedish parliament demanding stronger action on climate change. Soon, other students picked up the cause. By the time she addressed the UN Climate Change Conference in 2018, strikes were happening every week—around the world. For the UN Climate Action Summit the next year, she sailed to North America to avoid carbon-intensive flying. The challenge she issued in her speech still reverberates: "How dare you?"

The activism of Yousafzai and Thunberg illustrates the values of the generation coming into the workforce now—they want to contribute to the greater good and do not want to be part of a company or organization that puts profit above responsibility.

The COVID-19 pandemic forced many to work remotely, and at first the use of technology to do this presented a learning curve, but soon people adapted. Many experts say the nine-to-five in-person office requirement is in the past (if ever a workday in the corporate world ended at five).

Not all agree, of course.

JPMorgan Chase CEO Jamie Dimon, for example, said, "You have to look at the flaws of the Zoom world. It doesn't work for an apprenticeship program. It doesn't work for spontaneous stuff. Management by Hollywood Squares slows down honesty and decision-making."[13]

However, a hybrid system of two or three days in the office and the rest of the week at home will likely be the norm for quite a while for white-collar workers because that's what they say they want.

Here's why: Employees discovered they could work just as efficiently, maybe more so, in their home office, and without a two-way commute, many can enjoy more time with family or other personal time. It was liberating to be able to work from anywhere, untethered by the office.

Employers stuck on managing by forcing everyone to show up in person soon found out that employees would simply quit. They could find a job elsewhere, anywhere, and the post-pandemic market favored the worker.

You've got to adjust your management style if it's been the show-your-face imperative. It takes trust in your employees to do their job even if you can't be watching. The results will soon speak for themselves.

Probably harder is to build an esprit de corps among far-flung employees. Zoom calls or Microsoft Teams meetings can't replace the spontaneous conversations that happen in the workplace, the informal sharing of ideas and approaches that builds teamwork.

Let's be clear—as with so many aspects of managing, whatever you do to encourage teamwork must be genuine.

One company organized "Barefoot Fridays" with drinks at the office—a happy hour, if you will. One employee said she was told to "come back into [the] office for the culture." Turns out, she was the only one who came in; not even the HR manager who organized the event showed up. The employee took to TikTok to film herself in the empty office; soon it had hundreds of thousands of views, with many criticizing "office culture."[14]

On the other hand—and isn't there always another side to every issue?—remote work can lead to the notion of being available 24/7. Check your email after hours; shoot out an email as an idea occurs to you. Are you ever really off?

As a manager, resist the temptation for those middle-of-the-night emails. It's needless pressure; most messages can wait until the morning.

Making your staff feel like they have to continually check in via email can eventually lead to burnout. "Quiet quitting" became a buzzword in 2022, as burned-out employees put minimal effort into their jobs while perhaps looking for new ones or seeking downtime to recharge.

Remote, or hybrid, work forced a significant reconsideration of work–life balance. To be sure, it's not an entirely new notion. More women in top management positions in recent years have questioned why corporate life can't include childcare or flexibility for, say, a parent to see a child's after-school soccer game. As you have seen in earlier chapters, enlightened leaders like Indra Nooyi, formerly of PepsiCo, and Sheryl Sandberg, formerly of Facebook, have been speaking out on these issues for quite a while.

The quest for a work–life balance has moved beyond parenting—and that is good. Taking the time for a healthy body and mind translates to better productivity at work, which becomes reinforcing. A positive outlook can infuse all of your endeavors.

———

Another shift in the workplace—and a positive one at that—has taken root from social movements. I'm talking about diversity and inclusion. Though we have touched on this topic in chapter ten, it bears amplification.

First of all, these terms are not interchangeable. If you have diversity, that does not automatically mean you have inclusion. You have to establish, cultivate, and reinforce such a culture where everyone feels they have something valuable to contribute.

"If inclusion is not present, diversity may be achievable, but not sustainable," says Bernard Coleman III, global head of diversity and inclusion at Uber. "A lack of belonging adversely impacts an organization's bottom line through attrition."[15]

Vivian Maza, chief culture officer at Ultimate Software, notes that no one individual is responsible for creating an inclusive culture. "Your leadership team ultimately sets the tone for the entire company," she explains. "If you are in a leadership position and want to see change in your organization, first reflect on your own behavior and biases. Are you publicly praising all deserving employees for their outstanding work and providing recognition as often as it's earned?"[16]

Let's build on those points. Juliet Bourke, a human capital partner at Deloitte Australia, delineates six signature traits that make for an inclusive culture. Do you embody them?

Cognizance. Because bias is a leader's Achilles' heel.

Curiosity. Because different ideas and experiences enable growth.

Cultural intelligence. Because not everyone sees the world through the same cultural framework.

Collaboration. Because a diverse-thinking team is greater than the sum of its parts.

Commitment. Because staying the course is hard.

Courage. Because talking about imperfections involves personal risk-taking.[17]

Think about it this way. "Agencies have always brainstormed by pulling different people into the room: an art person, a media person, a finance person. Each person brings a unique perspective," says Drew McLellan, CEO of Agency Management Institute. "Similarly, companies should hire people of different races, genders, ages, and sexual orientations not only because it 'looks good' but also to encourage a wide range of perspectives. With today's ever-changing workplace landscape, that diversity of perspective is crucial for succeeding and staying ahead."[18]

That "pulling different people into the room" very well could mean a virtual room.

Despite the focus on diversity in the workplace, women still lag when it comes to corporate leadership. And this lag will widen, as women lost time in their careers during the COVID-19 pandemic when they had to school their children.

"We are backsliding," Bridget van Kralingen, former IBM senior vice president and lead sponsor of a study on women and leadership, said to Murray in his book. "If you are a CEO, you've got to get serious about this."[19]

Possible solutions include "better on-ramps for women returning to work, more flexible working arrangements, gender-blind hiring, and more childcare support."[20]

Positive, enlightened leadership is needed more now than ever.

What is the future of work?

Stewart Butterfield, the CEO and founder of Slack, which took off in the pandemic, doesn't like that phrase.

"There's better and worse uses of the phrase," he told *Forbes*. "I think the least constructive one is where the future is just something that's going to happen, where we're debating what will change as opposed to taking a more intentional approach and thinking about it as an opportunity to reimagine the way [we] work. People are making tweets or blog posts or articles that are speculating about what's going to happen to them, as opposed to them being actors in creating it."[21]

Be the leader you were meant to be, not a follower, not one who waits idly while someone else shapes the future.

CHAPTER 14

Share Your Power

Someone is sitting in the shade today because someone planted a tree a long time ago," observed Warren Buffett, one of the most successful investors in the world and a leading philanthropist. Since 2006, he has donated more than half of the stock he owned in his company, Berkshire Hathaway, a value worth about $45.5 billion.

As Buffett's remark implies, you may not always see the results of your generosity and thoughtfulness, but trust that the impact will be significant in the future.

To truly be considered a person of influence and power, you must share of yourself. There's a myth, or an ideal, if you will, that anyone can succeed by dint of their own hard work and initiative. But in reality, we stand on ground that has been ploughed by others.

Arnold Schwarzenegger could be forgiven if he thought he became successful in the disparate fields of bodybuilding, film, and politics on his own. After all, he came to the United States from Austria as a young man with very little. But that is not his view.

"People always say I'm a self-made man. But there is no such thing. Leaders aren't self-made; they are driven," Schwarzenegger explains. "I arrived in America with no money or any belongings besides my gym bag, but I can't say I came with nothing: Others gave me great inspiration and fantastic advice, and I was fueled by my beliefs and an internal drive and passion. That's why I'm always willing to offer motivation—to friends or strangers on Reddit. I know the power of inspiration, and if someone can stand on my shoulders to achieve greatness, I'm more than willing to help them up."[1]

I sincerely believe that being an enlightened human being includes an obligation to help others. That help can take many forms, as Schwarzenegger conveys.

In this chapter, you will see ways to share your power. It is not all about making charitable financial donations, though that is fine if you can do so. It is about using your creativity, imagination, and resources.

I'd like to tell you about two people in particular who helped me at a critical time in my life. Their mentorship styles took different forms.

I went to Walter Wriston, then the CEO at Citicorp and one of the most powerful executives in the world. I told him I had achieved a lot in my life but that I wanted to achieve more. I wanted to make a significant impact. He said he would find four or five people willing to give me advice. I ended up meeting twenty different people, from vice presidents on down. Hard-edged businesspeople.

One of the best kernels of advice Wriston gave me was don't try to do anything more than you can. In other words, don't overpromise. That was very helpful. Here he was, a leading financial expert of all time, taking the time to encourage me. I met him only twice and a year later thanked him; he was very gracious. I owe my success to Wriston.

Because of him and his calls, Dun & Bradstreet and J. Peter Grace, president of the diversified chemical company W. R. Grace & Company, became clients. Grace was one of the longest-serving CEOs of a public company, with forty-eight years as president.

The best advice Grace ever game me? "Always run scared."

The other person who helped me at a critical time in my life is Henry Kissinger, the diplomat and statesman. He might also be the smartest person in the room, but he's much more than that. He uses his celebrity to help people, not just in government. He uses it to advance people.

Kissinger talked about sensitive matters of life. Have a plan. One of the things you need to do, he advised, is to get your ideas out there. Some may agree with you; if not, then listen.

Kissinger is a content guy; Wriston was a contact guy. Both types of mentoring were invaluable. I'd never had anybody work with me like that.

Find a Kissinger or a Wriston in your life. Or be one.

As you advance on your path to power and influence, you should be mentoring others. It is necessary to help others; it's good for you and beneficial to your company or organization.

How to be an effective mentor? Well, it's not about meeting once a month and bestowing all your wisdom on your mentee. Sure, it's tempting to tell someone what they ought to do. But that's not your role, nor is it effective.

You must listen. What is it that your mentee wants to achieve? (If you are the mentee, have this clear in your mind before you begin.) Ask questions. What motivates them? What are their values?

"Much like coaching, mentoring is about guiding and empowering, not directing," advises Sheryl Lyons, founder and president of Houston-based Culture Spark. "Making the mentee the star—giving encouragement, helping identify skills and resources they both have and need, exploring ideas to reach their goals—is more meaningful than being prescriptive."[2]

Share your experiences and describe how you responded to challenges, but don't try to solve their problems. Rather, ask guiding questions that will lead them to find their own solutions.

Sheryl Sandberg, the former COO of Facebook (now under the parent company Meta), writes about the importance of mentors and sponsors in her book *Lean In* and importantly draws attention to the disparate experiences of men and women.

"Mentorship and sponsorship are crucial for career progression. Both men and women with sponsors are more likely to ask for stretch assignments and pay raises than their peers of the same gender without sponsors. Unfortunately for women, men often have an easier time acquiring and maintaining these relationships,"[3] she writes.

"Because it is harder for young women to find mentors and sponsors, they are taking a more active role in seeking them out. While normally I applaud assertive behavior, this energy is sometimes misdirected. No matter how crucial these connections are, they probably won't develop from asking a stranger, 'Will you be my mentor?' *The strongest relationships spring out of a real and often earned connection felt by both sides.*"[4]

The emphasis on that last sentence is mine. While crucial and true, be open to mentoring women (and I'm saying this to women leaders, too) and others underrepresented at the top levels.

Sandberg took mentoring to a whole new concept outside the office. In trying to help other women reach the heights of leadership and be comfortable with it, she initiated Lean In Circles, mentioned in chapter two.

Sandberg noticed a need and used her power and influence to do something about it. Within a few years, Lean In Circles spread to more than 180 countries.

Lin-Manuel Miranda, who broke records and barriers with his hit play *Hamilton*, sees mentoring as a continuum.

"I was inspired to start writing by Jonathan Larson," he says of the late author of the Pulitzer- and Tony-winning musical *Rent*, among others. "Jonathan Larson was generously mentored by Stephen Sondheim, who's mentored countless generations of writers."[5] Sondheim himself had been mentored by Oscar Hammerstein II.

"There is a way in which we're all links in the chain,"[6] Miranda says.

And Miranda insists on another way to share his power. A Puerto Rican, he wanted to open more Broadway opportunities to actors underrepresented on the stage.

Thus in *Hamilton*, which opened in 2015, key characters such as George Washington, Thomas Jefferson, and Angelica Schuyler were played by Black actors. Miranda himself initiated the lead role of Alexander Hamilton and performed it for many years.

Something beautiful happened. Not only did more ethnicities gain the chance to perform on Broadway; the audience also saw American history in a different light. The groundbreaking rap musical became wildly successful.

James Patterson, the bestselling author, shares his power in another way. He speaks to elementary-school students about the joy of reading. He supports independent bookstores by autographing copies of his books to sell. During the COVID-19 pandemic, he donated half-a-million dollars to help keep independent bookstores afloat and partnered with Reese Witherspoon, the American Booksellers Association, and others to promote the #SaveIndieBookstores campaign.

"I can't imagine anything more important right now, in terms of the book world, than helping indies survive,"[7] Patterson told the *Los Angeles Times*. He shares his wealth, too. In 2022 alone, he gave $5.3 million in cash awards to PEN America, Scholastic Book Clubs for classrooms, a dozen writer-education scholarships in his name at Howard University, and fourteen fellowships in fiction and poetry for the Iowa Writers' Workshop.

All these efforts dovetail with his life's work.

It's a great feeling when you can share your power and influence in authentic ways.

Maybe for you, it's sharing your money, your influence, your information or time, but whatever it is, you will be fulfilling a higher purpose.

CHAPTER 15

Power, Influence,
and You

Now that you have power and influence, have your notions of what the terms mean and how to use them changed? Are you thinking more outward than inward?

You do need to examine inward first—your values, your character, your dreams—before you can be an effective, positive force in the world around you.

Will you use your power for personal gain or for the greater good? Do you have the power to lord it over others or the power to make things happen that will benefit many?

The way you use your power says a lot about your character and will determine your legacy.

Influence is a way to direct your power. The term has been diluted to meaning who can get the most likes or brand endorsements or get others to follow the trends they set. This "influence" is not lasting.

Dr. Zoe Chance, an author, researcher, and professor at the Yale School of Management, has a concrete way to find your "influence superpower,"[1] as she puts it.

Her secret is a question that she claims can "transform conversational dynamics": *What would it take for us to resolve this?*[2]

"The idea is that this question, which should be tailored to each unique conversation and context, encourages a collective problem-solving approach," writes Kwame Christian, a contributing writer for *Forbes*. "As opposed to 'me versus you' it becomes 'me and you versus the problem.'"[3]

I mention this management tip here, at this point in the book, because it transcends the workplace. Imagine the progress there would be if every issue, personal or international, were approached with problem-solving instead of conflict. This dovetails to my earlier advice about assuming the best of others.

I have learned some simple truths. One is that the key to having influence is to get people to focus on a problem that is clearly and succinctly stated (and usually, you'll have to be the one to do the clarifying and the stating). Then, you find out why the issue is so emotionally important to the people involved; and finally, you offer a solution that satisfies all the parties needed to make the solution work.

Because we learn and remember best through stories (recall chapter six), I'd like to share this anecdote from when I was ten years old in the fifth grade at Our Lady of Victory.

In those days, there was no eating meat on Fridays and no food before the day's Holy Communion. Fasting was tough, so as soon as Mass was over, we would rush downstairs, where ladies from the parish would sell us a cup of hot chocolate and a doughnut (for the princely sum of fifteen cents), and, thus revived, we were able to last until lunch.

The nuns, though, decided our mad dash took too much time and created a disturbance. So they lobbied the priest, and the decree came down: no more snacks.

With the perfect logic of ten-year-olds, we did the one thing that would most bother the nuns: we stopped going to Communion. It was a stalemate that clearly needed a compromise.

I organized a group of students to meet with the priest and proposed this: Instead of racing up and down the stairs, we would buy the hot chocolate and dough-nuts from a hallway table we had to pass on the way back to our rooms. That way, the nuns would get us to Com-munion, the ladies would get their money, and we would get our beloved doughnuts!

It worked. Not always can all parties be happy with a resolution, but then again, not every roadblock is insurmountable.

Influence should be about inspiration. Inspire the best in yourself—at any age—and, by extension, in others.

This can look like believing in yourself. Be willing to take risks.

Levi Conlow was twenty-two when he talked his father into investing $50,000 from his retirement savings into his son's venture: an electric bicycle. His first version flopped. Not to be deterred, Conlow tried again and created a new model that in 2019 would sell at half the cost of a typical e-bike, which can cost more than $2,000. His company, Lectric eBikes, has sold more than 100,000 bikes and was expected to reap $85 million in revenue in 2022, putting him on *Forbes*'s 30 Under 30 list for that year.

"We got my old man paid back, and he's happy with the investment now," Conlow says.[4]

Celeste Ng didn't think during her early years that being a writer was something she could do as a full-time job. "It wasn't until I started working in publishing and I realized that really wasn't the job for me that a mentor said, 'You keep saying that writing is going to be on the side. Why don't you try and switch it?' I looked at my savings and I went, 'Okay, I need to try this,'" she explained in a 2018 interview with Shondaland. "I went to grad school and then I said, 'I have this amount of time that I can afford to try and finish drafts of a novel and if I can't, then I'll have to figure out something else to do.'"[5]

She didn't end up needing a plan B. Ng's first novel, *Everything I Never Told You*, was critically acclaimed and placed first in Amazon's 2014 Best Books of the Year list. Three years later, her novel *Little Fires Everywhere* became a bestseller.

Note that it was a mentor who gave her the nudge.

Soichiro Honda believed in himself, despite rejection when Toyota turned him down for an engineering position. He didn't give up. He began making scooters at home and found customers. He went on to found Honda, one of the most successful automakers.

His advice? "Success represents the 1 percent of your work which results from the 99 percent that is called failure."

You have the power and the influence to do good in the world, whether it's for individuals who believe in their vision or for the community at large.

Allan E. Goodman, president and CEO of the prestigious Institute of International Education, described to me how he viewed power players and their ability to respond to situations.

"They are not impressed with power, and they are not concerned with power. They are concerned with ideas and impact," he told me. "How you make the world less dangerous, how you make your community a better place, how you energize people to get their ideas, because you don't have all the ideas yourself. The best leaders focus on getting the best ideas and then doing something with them."

Look outward. How can you make others see their potential and reach it? The best teachers see something in the student that the student wishes were there, whether it's creativity, or smarts, or something that makes them unique.

Look inward. Where do you want your life to go? Be open to serendipity.

"I've learned that it is near impossible to predict the exact course of your own life or career, let alone that of the world at large," says Klaus Schwab, the founder and executive chairman of the World Economic Forum. "It is better to approach your life and career one small decision at a time and always with a positive mindset. This approach will pay off over time."[6]

Look back. Ask yourself: What happened because I showed up?

ACKNOWLEDGMENTS

Throughout my career I have been privileged to work with some of the best and brightest in their particular industry, including many Fortune 100 CEOs.

It is through these interactions and the give and take of ideas, thoughts, and suggestions that the ability to see how power and influence are best used began to really take hold in my business career. But the qualities of using power and influence can also translate into our personal lives and that is truly an art.

There are so many who helped with this book, starting with Jacqueline Smith, a friend and colleague who sat with me for many hours helping to shape this book and doing a great deal of research; to Joan Avagliano, whom I have worked with for decades and who always keeps my writing projects and so much more on track; to Matt Holt, my publisher, who welcomed this book into his imprint, and provided terrific insights and direction.

ACKNOWLEDGMENTS

Throughout my career, my wife, Jan, has been there to support me at every turn and provides a unique perspective which allows me to always get to the proper solution. She is my inspiration in many of my endeavors.

I would be remiss without thanking Nicholas DiMeglio, Nataliya Lustig, Francine Benedetti, and Mirella DeMoura, whom I work with virtually every day and who enable me to focus on what you have read in this book.

NOTES

INTRODUCTION

1 Morgan Hines, "Time to Have 'The Next Generation Step In': Carnival Corp.'s Arnold Donald Stepping Down from CEO Role," *USA Today*, July 31, 2022, https://www.usatoday.com/story/travel/cruises/2022/07/31/carnival-corp-ceo-arnold-donald-steps-down/10030121002/.

2 "The Global Cruise Industry: Hope for 2023," Institute of Shipping Economics and Logistics, accessed November 22, 2022, https://www.isl.org/en/news/the-global-cruise-industry-hope-2023.

3 Ray Dalio, *Principles* (New York: Simon & Schuster, 2017).

4 Dalio, *Principles*.

5 Teri Evans, "14 Things You Didn't Know About Mashable's Pete Cashmore," *Globe and Mail*, May 26, 2011, https://www.theglobeandmail.com/report-on-business/small-business/sb-managing/14-things-you-didnt-know-about-mashables-pete-cashmore/article4260668/.

6 Indra Nooyi, *My Life in Full: Work, Family, and Our Future* (New York: Portfolio, 2021).

7 Nooyi, *My Life in Full*.

8 Nooyi, *My Life in Full*.

CHAPTER 1: TAKING FIRST STEPS CRITICAL TO YOUR FUTURE

1 Dan Stifter, "'First Rule of Leadership: Everything Is Your Fault.' Hopper, *A Bug's Life*," University of Missouri–Kansas City Henry W. Block School of Management website, April 24, 2019, https://bloch.umkc.edu/posts/2019/april/first-rule-of-leadership-everything-is-your-fault.-hopper,-a-bugs-life.html.

2 Stifter, "'First Rule of Leadership: Everything Is Your Fault.'"

3 "Rita Moreno Reflects on Anita, Awards and Accents," NPR, March 7, 2013, https://www.npr.org/2013/03/10/173726066/rita -moreno-reflects-on-anita-awards-and-accents.

4 Janet Jensen bio page, The Jensen Project website, accessed November 28, 2022, https://www.thejensenproject.org/leadership /janet-jensen/.

5 Janet Jensen bio page.

6 Dalio, *Principles.*

7 Dalio, *Principles.*

CHAPTER 2: NETWORKING: YOU HAVE TO DO IT

1 Frank Bennack, *Leave Something on the Table: And Other Surprising Lessons for Success in Business and Life* (New York: Simon & Schuster, 2019).

2 Bennack, *Leave Something on the Table.*

3 Bennack, *Leave Something on the Table.*

4 "About Circles: What They Are and How to Lead Your Own," Lean In website, accessed November 29, 2022, https://leanin.org /circles-guide#!.

5 Don Spetner, "The Favor Bank," USC Annenberg Relevance Report, USC Annenberg School for Communication and Journalism, January 8, 2018, https://annenberg.usc.edu/research/center -public-relations/usc-annenberg-relevance-report/favor-bank.

6 Spetner, "The Favor Bank."

CHAPTER 3: THE POWER OF THE PERSONAL CONNECTION

1 "Bob Strauss—'Hell, Mr. President, I Didn't Even Vote for You,'" Association for Diplomatic Studies and Training, accessed November 29, 2022, https://adst.org/oral-history/fascinating -figures/bob-strauss-hell-mr-president-i-didnt-even-vote-for -you-you-dont-want-me/.

CHAPTER 4: THE POWER OF HELPING OTHERS

1 Mike Anthony, "This UConn Graduate from Hartford Is Making the Largest Donation in School History," *CT Insider,* October 14, 2022, https://www.ctinsider.com/sports/uconn/article/UConn -graduate-from-Hartford-makes-largest-17507427.php.

2 Anthony, "This UConn Graduate from Hartford."

CHAPTER 5: SOCIAL MEDIA: MAKE IT WORK FOR YOU

1 Sapna Maheshwari, "She Was a Candidate to Lead Levi's. Then She Started Tweeting," *New York Times*, March 25, 2022, https://www.nytimes.com/2022/03/25/business/levis-jen-sey.html.

2 Jennifer Sey, "How I Was Bullied Out of My Top Job at Levi's by the Intolerant Woke Mob," *New York Post*, February 14, 2022, https://nypost.com/2022/02/14/how-i-was-bullied-out-of-levis-by-the-intolerant-woke-mob/.

3 Sree Sreenivasan, "How to Use Social Media in Your Career," *New York Times*, accessed November 30, 2022, https://www.nytimes.com/guides/business/social-media-for-career-and-business.

4 Sreenivasan, "How to Use Social Media in Your Career."

5 Shel Holtz, "Social Media: Evolving Best Practices for PR Practitioners," in *The Public Relations Handbook*, ed. Robert L. Dilenschneider (Dallas: BenBella Books, 2022).

6 Sreenivasan, "How to Use Social Media in Your Career."

7 Twitter, "Permanent Suspension of @realDonaldTrump," Twitter blog site, January 8, 2021, https://blog.twitter.com/en_us/topics/company/2020/suspension.

8 Billy Perrigo, "Thousands Have Joined Mastodon Since Twitter Changed Hands. Its Founder Has a Vision for Democratizing Social Media," *TIME*, November 8, 2022, https://time.com/6229230/mastodon-eugen-rochko-interview/.

CHAPTER 6: YOU CAN BE A GREAT COMMUNICATOR IN EVERY WAY

1 "The Class of 2022: The Job Market Outlook for Grads," ZipRecruiter, accessed November 30, 2022, https://www.ziprecruiter.com/grad-report.

2 Nick Morgan, "How to Become an Authentic Speaker," *Harvard Business Review*, November 2008, https://hbr.org/2008/11/how-to-become-an-authentic-speaker.

3 Deborah Tannen, "The Power of Talk: Who Gets Heard and Why," *Harvard Business Review*, September–October 1995, https://hbr.org/1995/09/the-power-of-talk-who-gets-heard-and-why.

4 Frank Luntz, *Words That Work: It's Not What You Say, It's What People Hear* (New York: Hyperion, 2007).

5 John Hamm, "The Five Messages Leaders Must Manage," *Harvard Business Review*, May 2006, https://hbr.org/2006/05/the-five-messages-leaders-must-manage.

6   Hamm, "The Five Messages Leaders Must Manage."

7   Jeff Morganteen, "HP's Meg Whitman: One of My 'Big Failures' at eBay," CNBC, April 29, 2014, https://www.cnbc.com/2014/04/29/hps-meg-whitman-one-of-my-big-failures-at-ebay-cnbc-25.html#.

8   Tannen, "The Power of Talk."

9   Morgan, "How to Become an Authentic Speaker."

10 Morgan, "How to Become an Authentic Speaker."

11 Morgan, "How to Become an Authentic Speaker."

12 "We Make First Impressions in Less than a Second—How to Perfect Yours," *Today*, January 15, 2018, https://www.today.com/health/first-impressions-how-perfect-yours-t121162.

CHAPTER 7: THE RIGHT WAY TO MAKE YOUR MISTAKES

1   "Winfrey's Commencement Address," *Harvard Gazette*, May 31, 2013, https://news.harvard.edu/gazette/story/2013/05/winfreys-commencement-address/.

2   Aaron Taube, "What 11 Extremely Successful People Learned from Failure," *Business Insider*, September 9, 2014, https://www.businessinsider.com/what-successful-people-learned-from-failure-2014-9.

3   Taube, "What 11 Extremely Successful People Learned from Failure."

4   Eugene Kim, "Amazon CEO Jeff Bezos Explains Why the Fire Phone Disaster Was Actually a Good thing," *Business Insider*, May 18, 2016, https://www.businessinsider.com/jeff-bezos-why-fire-phone-was-a-good-thing-2016-5.

5   Jeff Bezos, 2015 Letter to Shareholders, Amazon, PDF file, accessed December 1, 2022, https://s2.q4cdn.com/299287126/files/doc_financials/annual/2015-Letter-to-Shareholders.PDF.

CHAPTER 8: WHEN TO PIVOT IN YOUR CAREER

1   Beth Castle, "Pivot! 7 Women on the Career Changes That Have Shaped Their Trajectories," InHerSight, January 26, 2022, https://www.inhersight.com/blog/career-trajectories/women-making-multiple-career-changes.

2   Robin Hilmantel, "Ina Garten: I Don't Believe in Making Goals," *TIME*, February 4, 2016, https://time.com/4198968/ina-garten-making-goals/.

3 Hilmantel, "Ina Garten."
4 Molly Savard, "Kim Malek's Sweet Success," Shondaland, July 30, 2018, https://www.shondaland.com/live/a22253835/kim -maleks-salt-and-straw-ice-cream-interview/.
5 Savard, "Kim Malek's Sweet Success."
6 Julie Ma and Brooke LaMantia, "It's Never Too Late: 25 Famous Women on Starting Over in a New Career," The *Cut*, March 21, 2022, https://www.thecut.com/article/famous-women-on -switching-careers.html.
7 Suzette Hackney, "Rosalind Brewer, Walgreens CEO, Says She's 'In the Most Rewarding Moment of My Career," *USA Today*, March 30, 2022, https://www.usatoday.com/in-depth/opinion /2022/03/22/usa-today-women-year-walgreens-ceo-rosalind -brewer-covid/9290781002/.
8 Paige McGlauflin, "The Number of Black Fortune 500 CEOs Returns to Record High—Meet the 6 Chief Executives," *Fortune*, May 23, 2022, https://fortune.com/2022/05/23/meet-6-black -ceos-fortune-500-first-black-founder-to-ever-make-list/.
9 Castle, "Pivot!"

CHAPTER 9: PROTECT YOURSELF AND YOUR REPUTATION

1 Jensen Karp (@JensenKarp), "Ummmm @CTCSquares - why are there shrimp tails in my cereal? (This is not a bit)," Twitter, March 22, 2021, 10:32 AM, http://web.archive.org/web/20220402045003 /https://twitter.com/JensenKarp/status/1374051365417230336
2 Cinnamon Toast Crunch (@CTCSquares), "After further investigation with our team that closely examined the image, it appears to be an accumulation of the cinnamon sugar that sometimes can occur when ingredients aren't thoroughly blended. We assure you that there's no possibility of cross contamination with shrimp," Twitter, March 22, 2021, 5:12 PM, https://twitter .com/ctcsquares/status/1374106771698032640 6?.
3 Melissa Dawn, "5 Positive Ways to Overcome Betrayal in Life and Business," *Entrepreneur*, October 21, 2016, https:// www.entrepreneur.com/business-news/5-positive-ways-to -overcome-betrayal-in-life-and-business/283686.
4 Don Weber, "How to Tell If Someone Is Manipulating You Based on Their Body Language," *Entrepreneur*, October 25, 2022, https://www.entrepreneur.com/living/5-body-language-signs -of-a-manipulator/436770.

CHAPTER 10: HOW YOU WILL BECOME A MEMORABLE MANAGER

1 Nicholas Carlson and Megan Rose Dickey, "12 Quotes That Reveal How Larry Page Built Google into the World's Most Important Internet Company," *Business Insider*, December 8, 2012, https://www.businessinsider.com/how-larry-page-came-to-run-google-2012-12.

2 Carlson and Dickey, "12 Quotes."

3 Dalio, *Principles.*

4 Kedma Ough, "3 Steps to Building the Workplace Culture You Want," *Entrepreneur*, October 3, 2020, https://www.entrepreneur.com/leadership/3-steps-to-building-the-workplace-culture-you-want/356908.

5 Ough, "3 Steps."

6 Ough, "3 Steps."

7 Nooyi, *My Life in Full.*

8 Nooyi, *My Life in Full.*

9 Phil Bohlender, "Why You Need to Become an Inclusive Leader (and How to Do It)," *Entrepreneur*, May 16, 2022, https://www.entrepreneur.com/leadership/why-you-need-to-become-an-inclusive-leader-and-how-to-do/423779.

10 Karen Horting, "What Role Do Men Play in Creating Diversity in the Workplace?", *Forbes*, November 1, 2017, https://www.forbes.com/sites/forbesnonprofitcouncil/2017/11/01/what-role-do-men-play-in-creating-diversity-in-the-workplace/?sh=1046abfd3578.

11 Elaine Thomley, "Opinion: Back to the Office? There's a Better Way,' *CT Insider*, July 15, 2022, https://www.ctinsider.com/opinion/article/Opinion-Back-to-the-office-There-s-a-better-17305327.php.

CHAPTER 11: THE INEVITABLE CRISIS: KNOW HOW TO HANDLE IT AND BENEFIT

1 Judith Rehak, "Tylenol Made a Hero of Johnson & Johnson: The Recall That Started Them All," *New York Times*, March 23, 2002, https://www.nytimes.com/2002/03/23/your-money/IHT-tylenol-made-a-hero-of-johnson-johnson-the-recall-that-started.html.

2 Jeff Bezos (@JeffBezos), "The news from Edwardsville is tragic. We're heartbroken over the loss of our teammates there, and our thoughts and prayers are with their families and loved ones," Twitter, December 11, 2021, 8:59 PM, https://twitter.com/JeffBezos/status/1469849245624647681?s=20&t=t1p Cz593QcE514v3laFpuw.

CHAPTER 12: PREDICTING TRENDS: YOUR KEY TO KEEPING POWER

1 Daniel Burrus, "Seven Radical Principles That Will Transform Your Business," HartEnergy, April 27, 2011, https://www.hartenergy.com/opinions/seven-radical-principles-will-transform-your-business-121410.
2 Brady E. Hamilton, Joyce A. Martin, and Michelle J. K. Osterman, "Births: Provisional Data for 2020," National Vital Statistics System Vital Statistics Rapid Release, May 2021, PDF file, accessed December 8, 2022, https://www.cdc.gov/nchs/data/vsrr/vsrr012-508.pdf.
3 Andrew Clark, "Farewell, Grand Caravan: Why I'll Miss This Minivan," *Globe and Mail*, May 7, 2014, https://www.theglobeandmail.com/globe-drive/culture/commuting/farewell-grand-caravan-why-ill-miss-this-minivan/article18508600/.
4 Burrus, "Seven Radical Principles."
5 Burrus, "Seven Radical Principles."
6 Nooyi, *My Life in Full*.
7 Nooyi, *My Life in Full*.
8 Nooyi, *My Life in Full*.
9 "How to Predict Future Trends and Transform Your Business," Enterprise League, April 7, 2021, https://enterpriseleague.com/blog/how-to-predict-future-trends/.

CHAPTER 13: HOW YOU CAN LEAD THE CHANGING WORKPLACE

1 "Leading in the 21st Century: An Interview with Ford's Alan Mulally," McKinsey & Company, November 1, 2013, https://www.mckinsey.com/capabilities/strategy-and-corporate-finance/our-insights/leading-in-the-21st-century-an-interview-with-fords-alan-mulally.

2   "Gartner Says U.S. Total Annual Employee Turnover Will Likely
    Jump by Nearly 20% from the Prepandemic Annual Average,"
    Gartner press release, April 28, 2022, https://www.gartner
    .com/en/newsroom/04-28-2022-gartner-says-us-total-annual
    -employee-turnover-will-likely-jump-by-nearly-twenty-percent
    -from-the-prepandemic-annual-average.
3   2020 Retention Report, Work Institute, accessed December 8,
    2022, https://info.workinstitute.com/hubfs/2020%20Retention
    %20Report/Work%20Institutes%202020%20Retention%20Report
    .pdf.
4   Bryan Robinson, "Discover the Top 5 Reasons Workers Want to
    Quit Their Jobs," *Forbes*, May 3, 2022, https://www.forbes.com
    /sites/bryanrobinson/2022/05/03/discover-the-top-5-reasons
    -workers-want-to-quit-their-jobs/?sh=56c72f475d46.
5   Jennifer Herrity, "5 Generations in the Workplace: Their Values
    and Differences," Indeed, May 18, 2022, https://www.indeed
    .com/career-advice/career-development/generations-in-the
    -workplace.
6   Herrity, "5 Generations in the Workplace."
7   Herrity, "5 Generations in the Workplace."
8   Herrity, "5 Generations in the Workplace."
9   Herrity, "5 Generations in the Workplace."
10 Alan Murray, *Tomorrow's Capitalist: My Search for the Soul of
    Business* (New York: PublicAffairs, 2022).
11 John Mackey and Rajendra Sisodia, *Conscious Capitalism: Lib-
    erating the Heroic Spirit of Business* (Boston: Harvard Business
    Review Press, 2014).
12 Lola Fadulu, "Not Everyone Can Afford a Job They Love," *Atlan-
    tic*, July 17, 2018, https://www.theatlantic.com/technology
    /archive/2018/07/reshma-saujani-girls-who-code/562055/.
13 Andy Serwer with Dylan Croll, "Jamie Dimon Sounds Off on . . .
    Almost Everything: Morning Brief," Yahoo! Finance, August 13,
    2022, https://finance.yahoo.com/news/jamie-dimon-sounds-off
    -morning-brief-110044236.html.
14 Melody Heald, "'Not Even the HR Manager Who Organized It
    Came In': Worker Says Company Invited Her to an In-Office
    Event for the 'Culture.' She's the Only One Who Showed Up,"
    Daily Dot, October 14, 2022, https://www.dailydot.com/irl
    /worker-asked-to-come-in-for-office-culture/.

15 Bernard Coleman III, "Inclusive Leadership: Just Be Good to People," *Forbes*, August 21, 2017, https://www.forbes.com/sites /forbescoachescouncil/2017/08/21/inclusive-leadership-just-be -good-to-people/?sh=3b9925201d67.

16 Vivan Maza, "Building a Workplace Culture That Supports Employees—Especially Women," *Forbes*, December 6, 2017, https://www.forbes.com/sites/forbeshumanresourcescouncil /2017/12/06/building-a-workplace-culture-that-supports -employees-especially-women/?sh=244a20471412.

17 Juliet Bourke, "The Six Signature Traits of Inclusive Leadership," Deloitte, April 15, 2016, https://www2.deloitte.com /us/en/insights/topics/talent/six-signature-traits-of-inclusive -leadership.html.

18 Drew McLellan, "Diversify Your Staff for Deep and Meaningful Results for Your Clients," *Forbes*, August 11, 2017, https://www .forbes.com/sites/forbesagencycouncil/2017/08/11/diversify -your-staff-for-deep-and-meaningful-results-for-your-clients/ ?sh=447d6ebd197c.

19 Murray, *Tomorrow's Capitalist*.

20 Murray, *Tomorrow's Capitalist*.

21 Jean McGregor, "Slack CEO Stewart Butterfield on Meeting Overload, a 'Dystopian' Metaverse, and a More Intentional Future of Work," *Forbes*, November 3, 2022, https://www.forbes.com /sites/jenamcgregor/2022/11/03/slack-ceo-stewart-butterfield -on-a-dystopian-metaverse-meeting-overload-the-future-of -work/?sh=71a2c049173f.

CHAPTER 14: SHARE YOUR POWER

1 Adam and Jordan Bornstein, "22 Qualities That Make a Great Leader," *Entrepreneur*, March 2016, https://www.entrepreneur .com/leadership/22-qualities-that-make-a-great-leader/299443.

2 Forbes Coaches Council, "Mentoring for the First Time? 14 Tips to Start Off on the Right Foot," *Forbes*, March 24, 2020, https://www.forbes.com/sites/forbescoachescouncil/2020/03 /24/mentoring-for-the-first-time-14-tips-to-start-off-on-the-right -foot/?sh=276a555121a1.

3 Sheryl Sandberg, *Lean In: Women, Work, and the Will to Lead* (New York: Alfred A. Knopf, 2013).

4 Sandberg, *Lean In.*

5 Donald Clarke, "Lin-Manuel Miranda: 'I Do Know What It Is Like to Be a Struggling Songwriter," *Irish Times*, November 20, 2021, https://www.irishtimes.com/culture/film/lin-manuel-miranda-i-do-know-what-it-is-like-to-be-a-struggling-songwriter-1.4730041.

6 Clarke, "Lin-Manuel Miranda."

7 Dorany Pineda, "James Patterson Donates $500,000 as Independent Bookstores Struggle with Coronavirus," *Los Angeles Times,* April 2, 2020, https://www.latimes.com/entertainment-arts/books/story/2020-04-02/bookstores-coronavirus-james-patterson.

CHAPTER 15: POWER, INFLUENCE, AND YOU

1 Kwame Christian, "The Secret to Influence: Ask the Magic Question," *Forbes*, June 13, 2022, https://www.forbes.com/sites/kwamechristian/2022/06/13/the-secret-to-influence-ask-the-magic-question/?sh=60ae0fa63c1f.

2 Christian, "The Secret to Influence."

3 Christian, "The Secret to Influence."

4 "Lectric Bikes," Lectric Bikes 30 Under 30 profile webpage, *Forbes,* accessed December 7, 2022, https://www.forbes.com/profile/lectric-ebikes/?sh=23a9b85b5660.

5 Melissa Hung, "Catching Up with Celeste Ng," Shondaland, April 27, 2018, https://www.shondaland.com/inspire/books/a19999462/celeste-ng-interview/.

6 Klaus Schwab, afterword to *Decisions: Practical Advice from 23 Men and Women Who Shaped the World*, by Robert L. Dilenschneider (New York: Citadel Press, 2020).

INDEX

ABOUT THE AUTHOR

Robert L. Dilenschneider formed The Dilenschneider Group in October 1991. Headquartered in New York, with offices in Chicago and Miami, the firm provides strategic advice and counsel to Fortune 500 companies and leading families and individuals around the world, with experience in fields ranging from mergers and acquisitions and crisis communications to marketing, government affairs, and international media. Prior to forming his own firm, Mr. Dilenschneider served as president and chief executive officer of Hill & Knowlton, Inc., from 1986 to 1991, tripling that firm's revenues to nearly $200 million and delivering more than $30 million in profit. Mr. Dilenschneider was with that organization for nearly twenty-five years. Mr. Dilenschneider started in public relations in 1967 in New York, shortly after receiving a BA from the University of Notre Dame and an MA in journalism from Ohio State University. Mr. Dilenschneider has been called the "Dean of American Public Relations Executives" and is widely published. He has lectured before scores of professional organizations and colleges, including the University of Notre Dame, Ohio State University, New York University, and the Harvard Business School.